Live Your Truth

and

Break the Cycle

Author:

Stacey Henry-Carr

Dedication

I dedicate this book to my daughter Chloe. Giving birth to you was the best thing I have ever done in my entire existence. You are my gift from God. I want you to always live in your truth. Be who you are to your core and make no excuses for it. Be happy with yourself from your hair follicle to your toenails. Your beauty should always shine from the inside, only then will people see you. Thank you for helping me to heal. I love you to the moon and back.

Introduction

"My mission is not merely to survive, but to thrive; and to do so with some passion, some compassion, some humor and some style" Maya Angelou

Growing up we thought that the enemy was the gun violence that plagued the streets of Kingston, and the poverty that robbed food from tables. The truth was that secrets were the enemy. This enemy sealed the lips of those who wanted to speak the truth. The truth that would have broken down the barriers and cleansed so many from the mind traps created throughout the generations. It is no wonder the darkness still exists. The roots run deeper than the four layers of the earth. It will require surgical removal of the thoughts on the brain of those who are afraid to utter the truth. The hypocrisy came with the words I was taught as a young girl. These words of "the truth shall set you free" and "speak the truth, God doesn't like liars." But these people, they kept secrets. Not just *any* secret--damaging and life-changing secrets. Did they not serve the God that didn't like liars? The web of deception was so thick that it clouded the minds of those who reveled in it and hindered their prosperity. The secrets were mixed with the paint on the walls; they were woven in the linens and the bedsheets; they were planted in the earth that grew the fruit trees.

They were the memories of ghostly shadows that haunted my dreams and later became nightmares and vague memories that made me question the actions. It was only with age and wisdom that I was able to see through the facade.

"Stace" was all the message said, but I knew something was wrong. I shared a very special bond with my cousin, and we know each other so well that I could hear her voice saying my name just from reading the text. It was the same tone she had when she wanted to make sure I still loved her when she became pregnant with her first child. "Nothing can change my love for you cousin." It was not surprising that she wanted to share with me what happened when a family friend sent sexually suggestive messages to her daughter. It was a violation that he would later regret. He must have believed that it would go into the secret society of sexual defiance that happened to so many before her. But he was wrong. He had met his match. He had encountered a mother who talked to her child and built a safe and trusting relationship. In this space there are no secrets, not when they matter.

It was with that one word, "Stace," that I knew that something important was about to be discussed. I learned that day that someone was in the fight along with me to break the cycle. The significance was grand because of where the incident occurred--it evoked a plethora of emotions from me. Not only was it because her baby was my baby, but also because she was at that "house." The house where love, shame, guilt, and hurt were wrapped in a blanket of secrets. But the result was pure satisfaction. I was pleased that my cousin was breaking the cycle, with her voice and her actions. She proclaimed aloud that "this stops with my children." And with that, the demons of the past that lingered in that space took flight, because they met their match. She was not going to be quiet; she taught her children to speak out.

She made sure everyone knew this was her children's life. Getting involved should never be an option for an adult when it is related to saving a child's life and breaking a cycle that has been a generational curse. The difficulty comes when no one wants to "get involved," or when the family's name is more important than the truth.

It not easy, because people don't want the exposure. This is when people make comments like "I knew something was wrong." Why did they turn a blind eye? What kind of issues will the exposure cause for them and others? None of that will matter down the line if silence caused hurt, and betrayal of trust to continue for generations. The family's name will not matter if it's built on lies and secrets. Then you are just a fraud, and nothing to be proud of. It becomes a shell with no substance of truth. It's a shiny coin with no worth.

 Child sexual abuse is a difficult topic for many. Most people will not venture into the topic. It is spoken about with a whisper in people's voices. But that raises the issue of why is something that needs to be out in the open kept so secret. Many people will not know that this book is for them. They might think they do not know anyone who was abused. Some people like a good friend of mine just gets so angry and cannot have the discussion. I agree that it is a heavy and intense topic, yet it is a necessary one.

This book is for everyone. If you work with children, have children, are thinking about having children, or just want to be aware. It is a call to action for people to be more vigilant and help prevent this type of traumatic incident from occurring to innocent children. Children should be given a fair chance to live a happy and healthy life.

I am a survivor of child sexual abuse. I don't like the word victim because it makes it seem like you lost the battle. I believe that if you can speak about your situation, if you can turn your mess into a message and help others to heal, then you are a survivor.

I grew up in Kingston, Jamaica, born to teenage parents and raised by my grandparents. The situation I grew up in was not the ideal family; it was far from functional, but it was the foundation of my existence. My formative years made me who I am today. I can champion boys and girls, men and women, and be an advocate that helps them find their voices. As I go through my journey of healing that started many years ago, I have met many other survivors and we created a bond of healing. We talked about breaking the cycle that was created generations ago within our families. We cried together, we laughed together, and together we found the strength to share.

The hardest part of writing this book came from the hurt I felt when others shared their stories with me. As they re-lived their pain, so did I. It also reminded me that everyone has a story to be told. I will share my journey from secrets to living my truth, which led me to bonding, and from bonding to breaking the cycle.

Contents

Part 1 Family of Secrets

Never Let them See You Sweat..................16

My Secrets..................25

Letter to My Mother..................33

My Baby..................36

Family Secrets..................43

Missed Opportunity..................57

Darkness of the Mind..................63

Cultural Disaster..................70

Finding Love out of the Darkness..................74

Letter to My Father..................83

Daddy's Girl..................85

My Decisions..................92

Regain Your Power..................98

Forgiveness..................116

Speak It..................113

Part 2 Bonds of Healing

Bonds We Created..................125

Tahlia's Story..................136

John's Story..................151

Blake's Story..................163

George's Story..177

Letter to Blake and George......................................190

Laura's Story..196

Kasha's Story...203

Stephanie's Story..212

Amelia's Story..216

Cara's Story..220

Part 3 Break the Cycle

Break it!..229

Interview with my Abuser...232

Recognize the Signs...237

It's Your Choice..244

Invest in Yourself...249

Use your Gift..254

Recognizing My Beauty...259

Replace the Doors...261

Your Sister's Keeper..266

Messages from Heaven...271

Step Out of Yourself..279

The Journey...287

Letter to my Abusers...291

Epilogue...296

Part 1

Family of Secrets

Never Let them See You Sweat

"The wound is the place where the light enters you"- Rumi

My appreciation for my birthplace came long after I moved away. Some friends and I went to visit, and we went as tourists. They loved it so much that they allowed me to see my country through renewed eyes. The beauty they saw was pure, because they didn't know the "truth." My roots, the foundation of my being, had more to offer than just the secrets and darkness that I had experienced. And so, we made it a thing. "Let's go to Jamaica" and we did. Awesome memories were made that helped me to tuck away the old ones. The ocean washed away the remnants of the past. The rum punch helped to numb the flashes in my mind and allowed me to become a tour guide for my friends. We celebrated as if there was something special about this place. But they did not know the deep-rooted secrets and dark past that I held close.

They come in flashes, memories of me as a little girl. Some of these flashes seemed a bit off-colored, and traumatic. I wondered why the good memories were so few in my mind's eye. As I think back to my young self, I felt sadness for the child who had no idea that life was not the way it should have been. I mourn the childhood that I did not have, but I celebrate the woman I have become.

I had been in pain for over thirty years, both physical and emotional pain. The summer when I turned fourteen years old was a time of big change for me. I moved from Jamaica to Darby, Pennsylvania, to live with my mother and left everything I knew behind. I was very excited about moving since I had always longed to live with my mother. My excitement was short lived when I realized that my mother had no clue how to parent a teenager. It was a struggle for many years. But one of the things that added to my challenge was the daily pain I started feeling at that age. At the time it was indescribable, but the pain felt like it was in my legs. After many years of trying to figure out why I was always in pain, and many years of just "dealing" with it. It had become my normal to feel this pain and to have a doctor's test not being able to diagnose what was wrong. It wasn't until after I had my baby girl my doctor and I figured it out together. I had Fibromyalgia, overactive nerves that attacked my body and caused me intense pain. If it wasn't bad enough that I struggled with post-traumatic stress disorder from my sexual abuse and abandonment, my body was in pain coupled with my mind. I was fourteen years old when I started feeling this intense pain in my legs and had no idea what it was. I remember being curled up in the bed next to my mother crying and not knowing what was happening to me. We made several trips to the children's hospital in an attempt for doctors to help me alleviate my discomfort, but to no avail. It wasn't until thirty years later I learned that my case was a classic one. Change of altitude and temperature with my migration from Jamaica to Pennsylvania, I had just started my menstruation, and Fibro ran in the family. I had aunts with the same symptoms. Had it not been for the open conversations I had with my aunt Jan; I would probably still be on a search for a diagnosis.

I still feel this pain from this incurable thing, yet I never let it stop me from leading a regular everyday life. I don't use it as an excuse even during times when I knew it was a hindrance. There is comfort in knowing that you can survive anything and rise above it if you just put your mind and actions to it. I am just realizing that the journey I have been on all these years was a difficult and painful one. For some reason I made it look easy, and it didn't feel as challenging, because I did it with a smile, a song, and dance. It was important for me to "never let them see you sweat," no one needed to know that I was in pain.

The shift to sharing came with my need

to help other people with their journey and healing process. I had interacted with so many people with a story that needed to be told. A story that they held close, yet when they spoke it left them feeling relieved. It was through these many interactions I started finding my place in this life I was given. I understood better why I needed to go through the pain. Now I can share, I can let others know that they too had a purpose for their pain that they were feeling. Through this ache will come to salvation not just for them, but for other people.

One day I was feeling sorry for myself, my body was aching, and my mind was clouded. I decided that after I dropped my daughter to school, I was going to go back to bed. I crawled in the bed and I put the covers over my head. That was short-lived, it was only a few seconds of what I called a "moment of defeat," when I busted into laughter and got up. What was I doing? I needed to keep it moving. Life doesn't wait for us to get up from our situations. In hindsight, I have had many similar moments, and there were times when I was not strong enough to recognize that I needed to get my ass up. But growth and maturity are wonderful antidotes to many of life's ailments. If you are willing to accept the challenge and fight the good fight those moments will be just that "moments."

Life keeps moving and we must move with it. We cannot allow ourselves to stay down for too long. I usually think about the many challenges' others are going through and have overcome and it made my issues pale in comparison. I am not insinuating that your pain or your issue is not important, but I can assure you that there is another person with a far more intense and traumatic story than yours. When I talk with others about their challenges I usually say, "you get the last brownie, you deserve it." I challenge you to rise from under those covers and use laughter, song, and dance during your moments of defeat.

My Secrets

I realized that there was always a deep motivation behind the things I have done in my life, whether good or bad. As a young girl, I had strong convictions about not having children. I was adamant that I would not bring a child in this world. At first, I was unable to articulate my reasons I didn't want children, but this strong feeling led me to have an abortion at the age of nineteen years old. I could hear my mother's voice saying negative things about my choices, and I could not imagine that I would get the support that I would need to go through something that was so life changing.

Because I came from a family filled with secrets, this became one of mine. It was something I only spoke of to very few, but the one person I wished I could have confided in, I knew I couldn't.

In hindsight, I was correct about not being ready. There were so many levels of myself I had not discovered and would need to get to know. The thought of abortion may go against what many people believe is right in the eyes of God, but for a nineteen-year-old college freshman with a dark past filled with sexual abuse, and abandonment, it was my only way. I only cared that God would forgive me. I often think what my life would be and what kind of mother would I be during that uncertain time of my life. It's important to know that not having a child was an easy choice at the time but became a hard pill to swallow later. It was during the process of writing this book that I reached out to the man who would have fathered that child and apologized for not giving him a choice. We had a healthy conversation about why I made the decision I did. I was shocked to know that I had shared all those fears and insecurities with him when I was nineteen years old. He was kind and thoughtful and left me with a validation statement of "time heals all. During this confusing time of my life, I knew one thing for sure--I had deep compassion for young girls, and I always felt that I wanted to help them in any way that I could. I knew I was in search of something in my life, that I had a void.

There were some missing links that only God and time would help me to fill in the gaps. During this time of my life, I remember leaving my university campus and visiting my late grandmother and we attended church. I was broken, sad, and wanted so badly to share what I had done. My grandmother was a woman with sight beyond what she could visibly see, so I am sure she knew. Her words were "child you are very sad," and all I could do was kneel in the presence of God and the woman who had raised and loved me unconditionally and cried.

My answers to the emptiness often came in my dreams. The recurring dreams of the house I grew up in went on for many years after I moved away. I was fourteen years old, well exactly one-month shy of my fourteenth birthday when I moved from Jamaica to Darby, Pennsylvania. I was very happy and could not wait to be reunited with my mother who left me during my formative age of one, in search of a "better life." I had dreamt of that moment all my life. I remember thinking it was going to be like the Huxtables. Claire Huxtable was the epitome of the mother I wanted and couldn't wait to embrace. What I did not know until thirty years later, was that my mother was a victim of a vicious cycle, and generations of darkness had plagued our family. She had not broken down the layers and peeled the onion of her mind. I realized over the years of self-discovery that I had to love myself before I could love anyone else. My mother had designer bags filled with baggage, and lacked self-love, and it made it difficult to embrace her mistake, that being me. My mother's story is not for me to tell. I can only share how I was affected by the lack of nurturing that I needed as a young girl. I was angry at her for leaving me behind. I wanted and longed to be where she was. I had a void but when I was given what I longed for I did not belong there. And so, I started longing to be gone again. It was the longest four years of my life. These were the years spent living in the shadows of my mother's pain and regrets.

Through my journey, I realized that everyone must handle their stuff in their own time. My time is now. Don't worry, this is not another woe is me story. This is a testament of strength, courage, and the will to break the cycle.

Living your truth doesn't have to be all about the bad things that happened to you in your life. For me, it's about how I overcame them and the truth about who I am, how I think, and why God allowed me to live this life. Sometimes we think we are here on this earth for our selfish reasons, but the truth is each of us has a purpose, and even with our ups and downs we are still destined for that greatness. You don't have to invent something spectacular. You don't have to make millions. You must open your senses to what your service to mankind should be. My real reason for living on this earth presented itself repeatedly, early in my life, but only through truth, honesty and willful self-discovery that I was able to finally say it aloud, and trust that it was my truth.

Letter to My Mother

Dear Mother,

I wanted so much to have a normal mother-daughter relationship. But I wasn't sure what that was until I gave birth to my baby girl. It was then that I realized how hard it must have been for a sixteen-year-old girl to give birth to a baby that represented everything that she was afraid of. I imagined you screamed inside "not a girl." That must have been the day you started saying, "I don't like girls." You said that often when I was around.

I wondered then *What did I do? Why doesn't she like me?* As I searched through life for answers to unlock our mystery the answers would manifest themselves. Since you never got a chance to forgive yourself. Since you grew up in that house of secrets where nothing was discussed, and everything stayed in the dark. In that house where bad things happened to the little girls. It took me a while to be able to see you and understand that you reflected the untold stories. It was then that I understood why you did not talk to me about the things that happened to me as a child. It would bring back the memories of the things you tried so hard to tuck away neatly in a compartment that had a key that was thrown away. I am no longer angry, and the hurt has subsided. The mean things you would say to me was simply your cry for help. Why didn't they help you? You didn't deserve any of what happened to you. You were made to grow up before it was time. You never got to experience the joy of childhood. The true spirit of falling in love with yourself and understanding what you were worth and what you deserve. Although I sometimes wonder who you are. What are the untold stories? I hear them in the silence of my mind, and I see them in your eyes.

With Love

Your Daughter

My Baby

When I was going through therapy for postpartum depression, I realized then that what I thought was normal was just me in survival mode. My daughter was almost two years old when I realized that something was very wrong with me. I was crying in the privacy of my closet and experiencing an overwhelming feeling that would take my breath away. I later learned it was anxiety and depression. I started to experience these feelings two months after my baby was born but refused to acknowledge that there was a problem.

When I found out I was pregnant I was very excited. I could not wait to meet my baby. I prayed for a girl. I called on all that the universe had to offer to send me a little girl. My husband and I had experienced a miscarriage just six months prior, and it devastated me. For a moment I thought I was being punished. But the truth is with a clearer head I knew better. God does not punish us, we punish ourselves.

After that disappointment I promised myself I would not give up. "We must try again." My doctor told me to wait for six months, and we did. I believe strongly that our daughter was conceived before or after the Tina Turner concert in Atlanta, Georgia. By that time in my life, I knew that strong legs and a stronger spirit could shake the rafters, and my husband and I both found her music an infusion of healing and light especially since she had walked through her darkness that ended with greatness.

Before to conceiving, I started taking better care of my body by eating healthy, I stopped using chemicals in my hair, and I took prenatal vitamins. I was determined to be healthy for my baby. This was the beginning of my journey of motherhood. I had a desire to be the best mother I could be. I wanted to give my baby what I wish I had been given when I was younger.

Since I asked, God delivered. I later found out I was having a baby girl. I was elated, but not surprised since I had seen her in my dreams early in my pregnancy. I read all the books I could find. I researched all the baby items that would aid in her formative years. I was a glowing pregnant woman with lots of love and support from a few trusted family members, friends, and coworkers. These were the people I had adamantly told that I would not bring a child in this cruel world. Now they were excited and could not wait.

When my baby was born, my aunt Jan was there to hold her and coach me through a very important, exciting, and scary moment. She stayed for over a year. To say I had support would be an understatement. There is no thank you that can express the peace of mind I had knowing that my daughter was surrounded with love during her early years. For as long as I can remember, my aunt Jan had always been a nurturing force in my life, so it was an honor to have her care for my baby

The day we took our baby girl home was when my anxieties started. I was packing up my hospital room and I felt my heart racing, so I called the nurse. I told her that I didn't feel well, she asked me to describe how I was feeling, and I did. She smiled and told me it was normal, "you are just feeling anxious." Since I had always been the pillar of strength for so many, I wasn't sure what she was talking about.

I couldn't imagine I was experiencing anxieties about taking my beautiful baby girl home.

The first night home I had the support of my mother, my aunt Jan, my sister Kiki (my daughter's Godmother) and my wonderful husband. However, it was then the struggle in my mind began. I took my baby to her beautifully decorated nursery and laid her down for the night, but as soon as I walked out of her room an overwhelming feeling came over me. I started crying and the tears wouldn't stop. "I cannot leave my baby alone," I said. Everyone tried to get me to understand that she was just in the next room. It was on that night I moved her to our bedroom. My husband understood my fervent need to protect our daughter. He understood my past, and the journey I was on. He did not know that night was the beginning of my depression and my worries beneath my smiles. It was that feeling of how I will protect her from the big bad world. This was the very reason I did not want to bring children into this world. But the difference was that I was no longer a nineteen-year-old college student who was completely lost and sad. I was now a wife, a mother, and a professional. It was nineteen years later from that child who was trying to pick up the pieces of a broken childhood. I was walking around in pain, masked behind fake confidence, and a well put together exterior.

Family Secrets

When you know that you're broken it is the beginning of a beautiful relationship with yourself. Only then you can start dissecting the inner workings of your mind to rebuild and rebirth a better you. Self-awareness is the start to the ultimate, which is self-love. In therapy, I talked about pretending to be strong. I talked about just wanting to be vulnerable and free of the burdens of trying to keep it together. My therapist welcomed my objectives and clarity about what I wanted to accomplish. As it was not my first attempt at therapy, I was adamant that this time I would lay it all out on the table. No holding back, let it flow, and surrender it all in the name if becoming whole.

It was during these weekly therapy sessions that I explored the recurring dreams of a house with doors that I would continuously try to lock at nights. The house was not a strange house, it was the very house where I grew up. These dreams were vivid as I ran from room to room amazed, and anxious that it was late at night and the doors were wide open. I would run to all four doors that led to the outside and attempt to lock them. It was always a chore as it seemed that I would struggle to lock these doors. I would sometimes try to lock the windows in the front room of the house.

This house was no ordinary house. It was a house built by the hands of my grandfather, and ran by my grandmother, and her sister, my grandaunt. It was also a house where many dark things happened but were kept hushed and in secret. No one talked about the molestation of the sisters done by one brother, and no one talked about the sneaky and destructive things that happened to the next generation of girls and boys including myself. Everything was hushed, and prayer was the way to overcome the monsters that came out of the closets. I noticed that these secret keepers displayed other people's downfalls and indiscretions with fervent pleasure as their stuff went unspoken and unresolved. It is as if to say I am perfect! Which is an attempt to hide from themselves and convince others that nothing is wrong. But the contrary is that it is a mask to suppress their hurt and brokenness. The sadness in the situation is that what lies deep within them is the truth that can help change the curse of a family.

As I continued with my therapy sessions it became apparent that the symbolism of my dreams was as straight as an arrow. The thing was that I was not safe in that house that I grew up in. The doors and the windows were wide

open for the intruders of my body.
These violators did not come in like a
thief in the night, they were welcomed
family members who masked themselves as
caring individuals in the day and
became my lifelong nightmare day and
night when no one was around. They were
the son of the grandaunt, and the
boyfriend of an aunt, and the welcomed
neighbor who smiled and respectfully
helped in the daytime. The protective
relative who no one would have
suspected in their wildest imagination.

If you are wondering why I would share
these indiscretions that are over forty
years old? Why would I open-up now?
Well it's simple, secrets will not aid
in breaking the cycle. Sitting around

with eyes wide shut will only damage the next generation. It is my duty to step up and help my mother to heal and speak so my daughter can understand how to protect herself.

What about the cousins who are unable to speak out because they feel ashamed, and guilty and have not allowed the cleansing of their minds and souls? What about the girlfriend who can't speak for herself, but can relate to my past struggles? What about me?

Healing has been a lifelong process, and through every stage of this journey I have found an outlet. I must encourage you all reading this book to speak up not just for yourself, but for others who can't speak for themselves.

Silence is crippling, and it will only leave you to survive. Don't you want to live?

As I continued with my cleansing through therapy and self-discovery, I realized that I had more control over this situation than I knew. As I dug deep in my subconscious mind and allowed vulnerability to take over, my fears about protecting my daughter, and being a great wife and mother were exposed. I felt broken and I needed to be fixed. It was like I was made up of puzzle pieces that needed to be rearranged.

As I talked through my junk, and unload my baggage, the realization of abandonment was as prevalent as my struggles with sexual abuse. I did not feel protected by my mother and my father because they were not around. I was surrounded by adults in the absence of my parents but none of them protected me from my body invaders. They reacted after the fact, when the damage was already done. Some of whom I thought were protectors, were victims continuing the cycle. Hurt people hurt others.

I remembered vividly watching a violent reaction to an incident that was discovered. It was a hot sunny day, and the household was buzzing. Looking back, I felt like I was having an out of body experience. My aunt was asking me questions, she might have even giving me a spanking. But the highlight of the buzzing was me traumatically watching my uncle beat one of my abusers within an inch of his life while the neighbors watched. I am not sure I completely understood it, because I was eight or nine years old. However, since I had been sexually molested all my young life prior to that episode, I am unsure that I understood the significance, or the seriousness of the chaos that was happening around me. I don't think I learned anything that day on how to protect myself from future episodes. I don't remember learning to make sure I spoke up and get an adult for help. I just saw violence.

Looking back and knowing what I know

now, it seemed like a mask, because the protector was also an abuser. He might not have abused me, but the deep wounds and scars that he caused was beyond any of our wildest imaginations. It was the kind of thing you only read in a book or saw in the movies. While everyone was aware that the little girls might be in trouble, they forgot to open their awareness to the idea that the little boys were equally in distress.

I have had some hard news and disappointments in my life, but none was as devastating as when I heard about Blake's secret of abuse. The reveal was a secret that he later shared had been plaguing his mind, body, and soul. A thirty-nine-year-old man had to share that a very close family member had sexually abused him since he was an innocent age of six years old until he was eleven years old, the very man others looked up to.

There were many taboos about the news: the fact that homosexuality is vetoed at the highest level in our Jamaican culture, and that I thought his abuser was my protector. At least that was the appearance this family member had created all those years. I had dealt with a miscarriage, break-ups, deaths of close and dear family and friends-- but none of those disappointed me like that reveal. For that moment it felt like my entire life was a lie. The people I knew were no longer the same people. They were upside down with twisted souls, and battered values. What was it about this information that had me doubting my very existence? Why did it feel like someone took out my heart? Why did I feel so empty? The emptiness had a lot to do with me empathizing with a six-year-old child who couldn't defend himself and would be put on the "hurt people's" list. I had been there, and I felt the agony that his mind must have experienced as he puzzled over why? As his older self, tried to brush it off and tuck it in a neat little compartment. As it rips at his soul and damaged his true self. I related so well that I grieved for him as I once grieved for myself. The problem was that the damage rarely stops with the victims. Often victims redirect their hurt to others.

As an adult I would look at my pictures from my childhood and my heart would get overloaded with hurt, and my eyes would express the loss. I would get lost in this grieving for a child that had missed out on having her parents, and whose innocence was taken away before she could speak her first words. I heard stories as I was growing up. Stories about how my abuser was caught "messing around with the baby." That baby was me. The room would get silent as I walked in, but my young ears already heard the damaging news. As an adult my uncle once shared with me that he threatened to drown my abuser until he shared all his indiscretions, he had done to me as a child. I don't think I needed that information it was emotional damage overload.

The point here is that they knew these horrible things happened, and yet this individual was still allowed to linger through the halls of the house. At one point he was moved to live in the back with the goats, pigs, and chickens, but that didn't heal his pedophilia ways. I am certain that I blocked out many things and shifted gears to be able to live a "normal" life. Because I don't remember many of the incidents in details, but I do remember the movements in the dark and being afraid. It wasn't until I was in my early twenties that I started having flashes of some of the things that happened. After being removed from the situation and allowing myself to think, it flooded my mind. It was a rough thing to navigate, especially with little parental support. I started worrying about the other little girls that were left behind to maneuver through this carelessness.

Missed Opportunity

One morning as I waited in my car until it was my time to go into my therapist office, I had a conversation with an older relative. This conversation shook me to the core, yet it helped me to understand some of the whys. She shared with me her deepest secret that came from the house we grew up in. She shared that she was with our grandmother, grandaunt, and my abuser at the local school while they cleaned up for classes to start. She was only a tender age of eight years old. She said our grandmother walked in to find the abuser raping her. He was beaten with a broom, and she was sworn to secrecy. As she told me the story I cried as I relived it with her. It all made sense to me why she had such a rocky life. In the classroom he took her soul, her joy, and damaged her mind for a lifetime. She shared that our grandmother asked her to never speak of it because she feared that her sons would kill him, which would send them to jail for life, and her sister would lose her son since he was the abuser.

That day my therapy session was a rough one. My therapist knew right away that something was wrong since I walked in with my eyes red, and swollen, and a broken spirit. Through my tears I told her the story. But that was the first time in my life I had ever expressed anger towards the woman who raised me. The woman who I idolized, and loved, I felt had failed me with secrets. How could she not address that situation the right way? Why was he not sent to jail? Why was she asked to hold on to such a burden? I thought the questions were never going to be answered because she was no longer alive for me to ask.

The significance of the incident was that my relative is eight years my senior. The cycle could have been broken, but it was hushed and left to continue. A cycle cannot be broken if no one speaks out about their abuse. I understand the guilt, and shame that takes over and makes it difficult to start the dialog. I also know the freedom of telling my truth repeatedly. I chose the latter, the more I shared the less control it had over me, and the easier it became.

Amazingly the heroes of our youth sometimes become our biggest disappointments in our adult life. This is no different from when we move away and return years later to see a smaller bedroom, or that hill that was too big to climb is now an easy feat. We have high expectations for the adults in our lives mainly because they always seem to know it all or at least that's what we thought. In their attempt to teach us right from wrong they mask their faults and all we see is a halo. The truth teller is age, growth and maturity that opens our eyes to things that we wished we did not see. Our idols and heroes are tainted and no longer wear their capes. The fall-out from this realization is a trail of disappointments and hurt. It is a very hard pill to swallow when you realize that your superhero is human. They cry in the dark and wipe their tears when you appear. What a disservice to my well-being that was.

We sometimes get accustomed to the way things have happened in our families to the point that wrongs start looking right. We allowed the passage of time to dictate the legacy of our name. But I say no more! I will birth a new normal and extend myself to show my children that I am not perfect, I cry, I hurt, I get depressed, I have bad days that aren't their fault. I am human and so are they. We are imperfect beings placed together by God, and he called us family. Therefore, I teach my children to strive for almost perfect because perfection is a myth.

I would have loved my parents to step up and say I didn't know how to parent.

I was young and scared. I made mistakes that might have caused you issues. Because in hindsight that is what I see. If you live with an open heart and mind your sight is greater than vision. You start knowing and understanding on a deeper level than you can even imagine. This was how I started seeing my true parents. I saw them as children lacking some basics that would have set a foundation for them being better parents. This was when my heart truly opened for forgiveness.

Darkness of the Mind

Who can you trust when the person that you thought was your protector was an abuser to someone else? We continue to teach our children about "stranger danger," but it is the people that share our genes, eat at the table, and show the world a family front that we must warn them about. It is those people who lurk in the darkness and inflict physical and psychological harm. I am sure that there are many stories that are untold because of shame and embarrassment, but the fallout from silence is far too damaging. Studies show that one third of victims of abuse go on to be abusers. Of course, there are numerous variables involved such as length of abuse and environment. But those of us who can acknowledge the abuse and start the life-long healing process will go on to be kind, helpful human beings who work hard to break the cycle.

I grew up in an era and culture where children were seen and not heard. I lived in a household where the adults were dismissive to the children. This was such a disservice to our growth and well-being. It caused secrecy that derived from fear and silence. It was worse for the generation before me. One of my aunts shared with me that she reported her molestation to her mother and grandmother on many occasions only to be yelled at and chased away. "You talk too much" and "shut your mouth." What a travesty that was? No wonder the cycle of indiscretions continued for so many generations. She was silenced, and no one wanted to talk about it. Maybe they thought if you didn't speak it then it wasn't the truth and it would just disappear. Like magic! That was a true form of denial.

I am not my mother! I am not my grandmother! I am not my great grandmother! I will not be silenced! I will make sure my story is told and not get bottled up like a distasteful preservative. The feeling of being silenced is one of oppression. It must be what my ancestors felt when they had to bow their heads and bite their lips. I say no to that tacit approach. Silence is not golden in this situation! I say yes to having a voice so loud that it will vibrate through the ears of the unborn children for generations. That would be a welcome legacy that they will be proud of!

When I was growing up no one around me talked about sexuality, or good touch bad touch. It was just something we learned the hard way. But I insist on talking openly and freely with my children about everything sex and their bodies. It starts with the awareness and understanding of how we support them. "You can tell me anything, nothing is off limits." I grew up in an unconventional family situation, born to teenagers and raised by my grandparents. This situation started my life with a huge void. That loss of parental bond, nurturing, and love created a feeling of uncertainty regarding my true self as I was growing up. I spent many days imagining what it would be like to be loved by my mother. I knew something was missing from my life, but since I never had it, I didn't truly recognize the gaps in my childhood until I gave birth to my daughter.

Throughout the years of being side by side and not missing a step of my daughter's growth, it was then that I realized I was robbed. Not only was I stripped of my innocence by way of sexual molestation, but I was left to navigate the world alone. I am sure you are wondering how a child can be left alone. I was left in the care of my grandparents who had to care for their children and other grandchildren. The living environment was crowded, and none of us were able to get the care we truly needed and deserved. Things went unnoticed and some things were just ignored and hushed. Since the adults in our lives neglected to talk to us about our bodies and the perils that lurked right in front of us, as children the abuse became a normal way of life.

Cultural Disaster

One of the things that I ponder now as an adult looking back to the homophobic culture that I grew up in, where were all the homosexual men? If they were all in the "closet" hiding from a culture that had zero tolerance for the lifestyle, what were they doing when no one was looking? Who were they doing this to? I cried for the victims who unwillingly spoke, but who are the others and how many are there? No child should have their innocence taken away from them, this rang in my ears as it came from someone, I was talking to who learned that the person she cherished and loved the most might have broken scared trust.

We must not turn a blind eye to abuse of anyone, whether it is against what our culture says is right or wrong. We never had conversations about homosexuals growing up because our culture was aggressive and violent to men who had a hint of "sexual abnormality". This lack of tolerance has a deep history and laws against "buggery" that carried on for generations. Anyone that was deemed to be gay lived in fear or as an outcast. People were killed for their lifestyle and that forced them into secrecy and caused many sexually deviant behaviors.

In my neighborhood there was a man who lived alone, never had a wife, only himself, then later his nephews lived with him. He was somewhat of an introvert, barely spoke to anyone, and all you saw was him coming and leaving. The only thing I knew of this man was that he was a tailor and he had the only telephone on the street for years. Forty years later and long after this man died, the whispers of his homosexual lifestyle floated to surface. They were relevant whispers as it was said that one of my family members who was later identified as an abuser, was in fact a victim of this secretive neighbor.

Then there was whispering about the Boy Scouts leader who had private photography lessons at his home for selected boys. The photography lessons were said to be much more sinister and would create significant life scars that might have contributed to a vicious cycle of victims becoming abusers. Later in life as my family member was living with secrets that he could not handle, he would say things such as, "I found out that my Boy Scouts leader was gay." It was that thing a person does when they want to share but are afraid of judgment and consequences---they drop small hints.

When you live in fear you cannot live with love, and without love your truth is lost. The problem continues in a culture that pretends that these homosexual abuses are not happening because they refuse to change their approach. In the household I grew up in it was much to do about not bringing "shame" to the family. The untold stories might not have brought immediate disgrace, but decades of lack of attention compounded the issues and left an unbroken cycle that destroyed additional lives.

Finding Love out of the Darkness

Not everything about my formative years was bad. There was also good, although the rotted wood caused my whole-self structure to buckle and sag in spots, there was also genuine love to buttress the foundational framework that made me the woman I am today. I learned early in life that family, education and God were important. It wasn't the conventional family--it didn't look like what I saw on television--but deep within the dysfunction there was love. My grandparents expressed love the only way they knew how since it's hard to do what you don't know. My grandfather told stories of running away from home at the age of fourteen years old because of an abusive father. Therefore, the love he was able to give was self-taught. My grandmother was just a worker bee, who spent her days being busy with raising her children and her grandchildren. It seemed normal at the time, but now looking back, it was a heavy load to for her to carry.

I also remember the richness of the earth as my grandmother gardened and grew food for us. I was right there handing her the tools and digging in the dirt. I have vivid memories of the fruit, and vegetable trees that surrounded the house. The mango trees where my favorites, but there were so many that I now know why I have a passion for certain foods. The papaya trees had the burnt orange color fruits hanging, while the sour sop tree had green fruits waiting to be ripen. We even had a grape vine that grew big purple grapes that were a treat when they grew. I remember the hibiscus tree at the entrance of our house where I often stopped to pick a flower for my hair. I have fond memories of going to the market with my grandmother as she bought the food we needed to survive for that week. I hated the market because it was crowded and smelly, but I loved being with "Mama." She loved the opportunity to show me off to the ladies at the market. I can still remember details of Carnation Market and can visualize myself navigating through the chaos. At our house we had chickens, pigs, and goats that would occasionally meet their demise for the sake of dinner. As great as dinner would taste, I did not look forward to the process.

The memories of my grandfather coming home after a week away from "work" and bringing with him the biggest bag filled with fruits, grapefruit, and oranges. I remember the reverence of my grandparents as they prayed for everyone and woke us up early each Sunday to have a prayer meeting in the living room before we would travel miles to a rough part of town for church. I used to wonder if God wasn't present in the many churches we passed on the way. These prayers were heartfelt and intense. My grandparents had serious joy and pain flowing from their mouths to God's ears. I never understood it until I became an adult and my eyes were wide open.

Love is shown in different ways. Not only do I show my love with my actions, I say the words often because sometimes that is what is needed. I didn't hear the words "I love you" growing up, but there were subtle ways that some of my family members would show that love. My favorite uncle would make certain that I had money for lunch before I left for school. I looked forward to seeing him in the mornings because sometimes he would take me to school, or to get my bus. He also brought treats like ice cream, or just a simple "did you eat?" My uncle showed love through his caring. His actions were more like a father than an uncle. But there was only one of him, and many of us. Although he was not obligated to do any of these caring deeds, his heart was open. He carried the burden of ensuring that his nieces and nephews were good. As an adult my mother told me that she asked him to look out for me while she was gone. I never knew that they had that conversation, but he lived up to his promise and for that I am thankful.

I have fond memories of two loving aunts. I remember the love I felt being around them and loved being in their company. Whether I was learning how to sew or just hanging around sharing my thoughts. I felt safe and loved when one combed my hair and place pretty bows on the ends. They taught me how to sew buttons and hem a dress. They were kind and always used kind words and actions. They replaced the mother that I was missing. Even as an adult I looked forward to conversations with them because I could share anything and still feel their love. When one of my aunts left for other country, and the other moved away it was hard, but our bond was a lifetime bond that allowed us to continue without a snag.

And then there was the food I grew up eating. I can still smell the red peas soup that was made in the outdoor kitchen on a wooden fire, stirred by a wooden spoon. There is a nostalgic feeling when I think of these moments. There was love in that pot of soup, and that bag filled with fruits. There was love with the gesture of bringing ice cream. There was love in the hands of the aunt as she combed my hair and showed me how to sew a button. That love is why I was able to move past the pain. It was that love that allowed me to return for many visits, and still felt like I was home. It was that love that allowed me to take my friends to visit the house I lived in when I was a little girl. It was that love that allowed me to take my daughter to a place that caused me pain.

Letter to My Father

Dear Daddy,

We are so much alike. I am happy to have been able to gain back some quality time to spend with you. It has allowed me to recognize me in you. I want you to know that the day you said "my daughter, I am sorry" the clock started over for us. Not because you said the words, but because your tears solidified the meaning. I am not sure that you understand how important you are to me. Every girl wants to have their daddy in their lives. At least this girl does. I don't really know your story, but what I know is that you are a strong spiritual being that did not know how to channel that energy as a young boy. No one had to tell me that, I can see it in your eyes. I forgive you for not being there, because you are here now. I understand that your actions were out of fear of losing your family, just to end up losing them anyway. But we are here now. Sometimes things just happen too soon. Sometimes we are not ready. But I thank God every day for the moments we spend together. They make my heart sing, and my feet dance. Your presence brings me calm. Your words of wisdom remind me that our souls are woven together by God. This girl loves her daddy. Let's continue to make up for lost time.

With Love

Your Daughter

Daddy's Girl

To add insult to injury, or as my late grandmother would say "put salt in the wound," my abandonment came two-fold. I was sixteen years old when my mother decided to send me and my brother to live with my father in Houston, Texas. I viewed it as another adventure since I had not lived with my father and thought it would be great to get to know him. As a young girl seeking stability and a place to belong, it was exciting. Considering my relationship with my mother was a rocky one, with no maternal support, leaving would be easy.

It didn't matter to me that my prior visits to Houston always ended with a false claim that I had stolen money. The accusations were indirect, but I picked up on a pattern and shared it with my mother. I never asked my then nine-year-old brother if he was the one stealing the money, but I knew for sure I wasn't stealing, yet I was being accused. I still overlooked the accusations and happily packed my bags and moved to Texas, where I thought I would spend the rest of my high school years living with my father.

The joy of living with my father was short lived, when the accusations became direct, and my father and his then girlfriend verbally attacked me about stealing their money. I was a sixteen-year-old child with nothing other than boys and clothes on my mind. I knew I did not have to steal my father's money because he gave me whatever I desired. I knew that my needs and wants would be taken care of. I also didn't understand why I felt so attacked. I started feeling like I was not welcomed by his girlfriend. Maybe raising another woman's children was going to be too much for her, especially since she had just given birth to her own. With all the accusations, and unwelcoming vibes in the house, I didn't even make it through the summer. I was ready to go back to live with my mother.

This did not go over well with my father. He was so pissed that I wanted to leave that he told me he didn't need me, and he would start a new family. Imagine being sixteen with a rocky relationship with your mother, thought you had your father on your side, and he said those words. The words came at me like venom from a snake. They pierced my soul, and at that instance made me a different child. As I locked myself away in my room, I planned my escape. I could not live here, I knew it would not be good, not when it started this way. My plan was a simple one that led me to climb out the window of my brother's bedroom and walked to meet my mother's friend who took us to the airport to catch my flight back home. That morning when I was leaving, I left everything behind. I took myself and my brother, because he was all I had. I spent many years agonizing about whether I made the right decision in taking my brother with me that hot Houston morning. It became a guilt that rested on my heart. I still struggle with that decision that I made thirty-two years ago. I often wondered how that day impacted my brother's life since we were left to cope with that experience without any parental guidance.

I felt like I was stuck between a rock and a hard place. My mother didn't want me, she had no idea how to parent a child who was the same age she was when she gave birth, and now my father was angry at me, and vowed to start his new family without me. *Where did I belong? What horrible parents*, I thought? *What a damn nightmare?*

It was during that situation I made a promise to myself that I would not be able to trust anyone but myself. My mother and father betrayed me twice. Now I was a sixteen-year-old girl more confused, and alone than before. I felt like I would have to navigate the world alone. I did it during the first stages of my life, and I knew I could do it again. But I soon found out that these beautiful souls that God allowed me to choose as parents before I was born, were not horrible parents, just lost individuals with emptiness, and voids caused by their own upbringing. As I stated before, my parents' story is theirs to tell. I have yet to get openness and sincerity from my mother about her life. My mother and I had a conversation once with the aid of a relative. But it was obvious that although we had a breakthrough that day, there were things my mother could not reveal. That day unveiled to me why she behaved and reacted the way she did. But there are still many missing links that time might reveal.

My Decisions

There are many fall outs from not having my father in my life. I was happiest when I spent time with him watching movies and talking about me not losing my "roots" as we listened to reggae music and talked about Jamaica. There were those times he took me shopping and fed the soul of a teenager with fashion of the 1980s. Although they were married, I never lived with my mother and father together. They were separated when I immigrated to live with my mother and her then boyfriend. My father had spent many years in jail for running a drug operation. My mother was left as a single mother raising my younger brother. The irony is that now looking back, I don't believe I missed out on living with them both, since the stories I heard was that of a rocky marriage. I also realized that my mother had not started her journey of healing, which can make it difficult for a marriage to thrive.

But as a young girl who felt alone and lost, not having a father didn't help my confidence. I didn't know my self-worth, struggled through some tremulous situations with boys. This lasted throughout my young life into my adult life. I didn't learn how to set boundaries because no one thought me how. I wanted the attention and using my sexuality, which was awakened in me from a young age, was the only way I knew to get it. I hadn't learned that I was a "pearl." I didn't know my value, nor that I had a light that shined from inside out. No one told me what I was worth--I learned it later. The good news was I had learned early to listen to my inner voice, my intuition, my spirit guides, my angels. And without that clairvoyant ability that came by way of my dreams, only God knows where I would be today.

My relationships were often with men that were unavailable emotionally and were unable to commit. It made sense now looking back that I attracted myself. I was emotionally unavailable and didn't know what I was worth. That energy brought to me those like me. If I couldn't share my true self with others, then I invited people who lied and cheated. It was not what I wanted. I longed for stability and true love. I now know I was in search of that love. I just didn't realize that it had to come from myself first.

I recall on a few occasions having the choice between the person who left beautiful flowers at my door, or the person who was evasive and missing. The absentee boyfriend would win all the time. There was safety in being by myself. I liked keeping my story hidden. I didn't have to worry about whether to trust these men because I already knew they were not trustworthy.

Not all my decisions were bad. I knew I had to take care of myself and started pulling on the strength of that little girl who grew up without her mother. I started pulling on the foundation that was laid for me by my grandparents. Education and hard work were my plan. I started setting financial goals for myself, worked through college, and landed my first job a few weeks after graduation. I wanted to be self-reliant and independent of my parents since I felt that they could not be trusted. I was twenty-nine years old when I bought my first house, had a master's degree and was ready for my next challenge. I wouldn't stop because I had something to prove. It was important to me that I was not viewed as broken, even if I felt broken. I worked in a job that provided me financial stability and allowed me to stay independent of the parents I did not trust. I was not going to be the things my mother said. She said mean things that could have shaped me into a different person. But there was something special happening to me amid these dark days. I felt engulfed by a light, internal joy, and happiness that even when I cried it was there. I now know that it was my destiny creating the internal strength so that I would carry-on.

Regain Your Power

Taking back your power is not about revenge. It is not like the movies where you wait in a dark room with the weapon of your choice for your abuser; it is different for everyone. I took back my power by talking about my abuse, sharing with other women whom I knew shared a common bond. I confronted my abusers, stood face to face and confidently asked why? I took back my power by getting married and starting a family.

Before my husband and I got married I shared with him that I did not want to have children. I told him that I had other children in my life that I would share my love with. I remember he looked at me and affirmed my declaration as if he could see deep in my soul. He knew something I didn't, or he just believed in the woman he was going to marry. Because two years into the marriage I was ready. I announced one day "let's have a baby." I remember the smirk on my husband's face as if he knew that day would come. The ability to be vulnerable and love freely and openly came with growth. It was a part of that journey I was on to be healed from my past. Having a child was going to be a huge piece of the puzzle. It was going to mend a void that I had been feeling for many years of my life before marriage.

I had taken my stepson home to Jamaica. It was October 2017, and when I got to my family's home, I found out that my grandaunt was in the hospital. My grandaunt was one of the driving forces in my life. She was a kind woman who helped my grandmother to run the household filled with children and grandchildren. It's important to know that it was her son that was one of my abusers. I was sad to hear that she was not doing well and quickly made my way to the hospital to visit her. While I was there, the reality hit me that I was not in a hospital in the United States with all its luxury. I kept looking around and complaining about the drab looking environment, with all these sick, and dying people separated only by curtains. I so wanted this kind woman that had served all her life to be in a nicer place. However, it didn't seem to bother her at all. She appeared peaceful, calm, and just happy to see me. She immediately asked me about my mother, and other family members in the United States whom she had not seen in a while. As I hugged her frail body, I felt the strength of her soul, and the joy in her spirit, but I knew it was just a matter of time. My favorite memory of that hospital visit was me trying to feed her some soup that we brought her, and her refusing to be "babied." She stubbornly took the spoon away from me and said in her broken dialect, "mi can feed mi self."

However, the significance of this hospital visit became more than just my sick grandaunt. Before I left the United States, I told my husband that when I got to Jamaica, I was going to confront my abuser. I told him it was time for me to take back control of what was taken away from me. I was ready to bring a child in the world and needed to address some things.

So, that which you put out in the universe with true intentions will manifest for you. As I was sitting on the bed with my grandaunt, her son, my abuser walked up behind me with his family in tow. He placed his hands on my shoulders, and with a childish grin said hello. I felt anger run through my veins, along with the devilish thought *I am going to kill you when your mother passes*. But that thought was quickly interrupted by a calm inner voice that said, "this is your chance to confront him." Now I am no saint, so believe me when I tell you that the many ways of confrontation that went through my head is left to your imagination. But in reverence of a woman who once took such great care of me, I handled it in a God like way.

I stood up to gain back my control of him standing over me. I said, "I need to talk to you." He looked at me with a nervousness as if he knew what was coming. If you have ever been to a hospital in the islands, some of them have balconies that lead from the wards. I ordered him to follow me to the balcony so that we could speak in private. At this moment I had flashes of my broken self, of his wife, and children that we left behind us, and bad thoughts of pushing him over the balcony came to my mind. Remember. I said I was no saint. However, instead of pushing him over the balcony, and becoming a fugitive in my own country, I handled it with grace.

"Do you remember what you used to do to me as a child?" The look on his face was one that said, "Oh crap.". He did not respond, so I immediately went into my speech. "Do you do that to your children?" He quickly responded, "No, I am a changed man now; I have been in the church, and the things I used to do I no longer do." I stood close to him and I looked him in his eyes, and I said, "Those things that you did to me were damaging, they hurt, and they ruin lives. I need you to promise me that you will not do that again to any other young girl." He nervously said, I promise that is not me anymore. I have a family." I said, "Then I forgive you."

As we walked back into the hospital from that balcony, I felt lighter. I felt like my thirty-six years of living had changed, I felt proud, and re-born. It didn't matter to me whether he was really a changed man, I am not even sure I believed him. But it was important that I forgave him.

I tried sharing my joy with my aunts in Jamaica, but none of them responded with the joy and excitement that I was feeling. It was a big deal for me. I am not sure they understood the magnitude of that moment, and the divinity in the situation. However, when I called my husband and shared with him, he knew the significance, and listened intently to my story.

There were other monsters that I had to confront, and I was not afraid. Another confrontation happened during the time I was in therapy when my daughter was almost two-years old. I called to get his number because I knew I needed to address it. To my surprise he called me before I could call him. It was a casual "Hello, what's up?" He was jovial and happy. "How are you? It's been a long time," he said. He had no clue what was coming. He congratulated me on the birth of my daughter, and it made me feel sick to the stomach. I didn't want him to mention my daughter. I instantly went into protection mode and started on my mission. "Do you remember what you used to do to me as a child?" He said "No, I did that to you too? I was always fond of you. I don't remember, but I believe you if you said I did it." His nonchalant, and cavalier attitude was revolting. I thought to myself, *how many were there?* He went on to ask me, "What did I do to you?" It was with that question that I knew it was time to end the conversation. There is no way I was going to help this sick bastard to relive his repugnant behavior.

It truly is not an easy task to tell someone you love that the person who hurt you was someone they loved. But it was a necessary part of a hard healing process. It was years later that I was able to share with my aunt what her boyfriend did. She was devastated. She cried and told me she was sorry. She tried to connect the dots as to when and how. I felt like I was consoling her about the incident. She said she remembered me saying things to him like "You are nasty," and that I would chase him away from him from me. What he used to say to me was "I saved you." The story he told was that he fought with another relative as he was attempting to violate me as a young girl. But later in life this disgusting human being would whisper in my ears, "I saved you." I know that the universe is waiting to give him exactly what he deserves. What my aunt did not share with me on that day was that she had heard a similar story from another young girl, her own daughter.

It was with that conversation that my aunt understood why as I got older I removed myself from her. I had to remove myself from the predator, even if he no longer had the power to hurt me. I realized then that my healing process was also helping others. My aunt was another part of the puzzle of secrets, and family members with their "eyes wide shut." She grew up in that "house" where everyone was silent, and things were happening around them that were devastating lives. This was the same aunt that took me with her to different places when I was younger. She looked out for me and in many ways thought she was protecting me.

I was around thirteen years old, and I had just gotten home from school. I was still wearing my school uniform--I attended Immaculate Conception High School. My Aunt asked me to come with her to take my cousin to see a spiritual healer. He had been sick, and no one could figure out what was wrong with him. We went to see this man, and I remember having to wait while they went in a private room. I am not sure what they did behind those doors, but I remember my aunt discussing the outcome. The spiritual healer said that demons were causing my cousin to be sick by violating him sexually. In hindsight that diagnosis was straight forward and for the life of me I cannot understand why such a big clue of abuse was missed. This diagnosis would turn out to be a devastating truth revealed decades later.

When I spoke to my cousin about what happened to him, I shared my memory of going to this spiritual healer with our aunt when he was "sick". He told me that our aunt had seen him crying one day and asked him what was wrong. He said he wanted to tell what her the truth, but out of fear he just told her that he was hurting. With that information our aunt decided to take him to see a spiritual healer. My family did not follow through with a doctor's visit, instead this spiritual healer was invited to our house to perform some sort of ritual. When you grow up in an environment of secrets and lies it makes it hard to see the truth even when it is staring you in the face. That was a big miss, and some would even call it neglect.

My abuse didn't all happen at home. There are places that you may think your children are safe and they are not. When I was around twelve years old, I used to go to the local YMCA to practice swimming. This was something I loved, and their pool served as that place to visit on Saturdays to brush up on my swimming. It was there that I met my first predator outside of my house. The swim instructor liked touching the young girls that he was hired to teach how to swim. To make matters worse one day while I was in school at Immaculate Conception High School, an all-girls school, my class was introduced to our new swim instructor. It was to my surprise that the same swim instructor from the local YMCA who preyed on young girls was hired to teach at an all-girls school. It seemed like there was no escaping these types of men. How many of these girls have stories to tell of the things this man has done to them? During my journey of healing I tried calling the local YMCA to find him, to confront that past, but was unsuccessful.

One day I decided to reach out using Messenger. "Good Day, you use to have a swim instructor named Todd. It's been about 35 years now. Just wondered what ever happened to him?" At first, I received an automated response thanking me for my message. About a week later I received a message that stated, "Praise the Lord, he is still here." I was happy that I got a response, but I was sad that he was still working in a capacity that gave him access to young girls. I wondered how many other girls he violated throughout the years. The thought of it broke my heart. However, I was not going to be silenced. "Well I am afraid I have to tell you that when I was a young girl attending the YMCA on Saturdays, I might have been 13 years old, Todd used to invite me to his office where he would touch me inappropriately. Seeking him out is not to praise him, but to make people aware of what they are dealing with. I do not want this to happen to any other little girl." The communication went silent, and I never got a response. I did my part and I prayed for the rest.

Forgiveness

I was taking an on-line training created by the Darkness to Light organization, *Stewards of Children,* and it was during this training that one of the survivors stated that she heard her pastor preach about forgiveness and it change her thinking about her sexual abuse. He said that not forgiving is like drinking poison and expecting the other person to die. That was such a powerful statement with a wealth of meaning. It was that statement that made me realize that when I said "I forgive you" to my abuser it was a release of poison from my soul. My heart felt like it was beating differently, and my work to help others heal and overcome consciously began.

Forgiveness is not an easy thing, but it is a necessary thing. I realized that I gave a lot of thought to my abusers prior to me reaching out and saying the words "I forgive you." I thought that once I released that negative energy from my heart, I would be a better wife, a better mom, and have more insight to help others. Through my journey, as I shared my story with those who needed to hear it, I would share about me confronting my abusers and that I forgave them. But it was not that easy.

Forgiving is an easy word to say. It

sounds nice and responsible. We say it sometimes without a true understanding of what it means. There are entire books on forgiveness. When I told my relative that I forgave him, I had no idea what those words meant. The words were orchestrated by my desperate need to move on with my life and be well. What does it really mean to forgive? We often say we forgive but still carry around deep resentment. Then we didn't truly forgive. I knew that forgiving him would not erase the memories of what he did. I knew that it would not truly change my hyper-sensitivity to the subject of sexual abuse. So, what was it for? And how could I truly forgive?

It was after I had a conversation with Blake, and he spoke to me with such humility and reverence about what blemished his soul so many years ago. As he spoke, he still had kindness in his heart and forgiveness in his tone. But all we wanted to do was understand it. We longed for the answers that ran deep in our family. We wanted to figure it out. What would cause someone to do the things that were done to us? It was through this exchange that I realized that I was going about this the wrong way. If I wanted to break the cycle, I would need to find out from the abusers what made them do what they did? What would make someone protect one person and abuse another? What was going on in their minds? That was when I said aloud, "Monsters are not born--they are created."

If we are to break the negative trend that happens in our families, we must get to the root of it. And what I know for sure is the root usually runs deep. The journey of healing shifted to a deeper understanding when I stopped being angry and moved my energy toward a better understanding of how to break the cycle by understanding the root. It was then I realized my ultimate healing solution was forgiving the person that my abuser was *prior* to his defining moment. The moment that someone changed him forever.

It was through this thought pattern and paradigm shift of my mind that the true healing began. I would not only heal for me, but for my abusers who was unable to take the higher road. Their path might have been different if someone had stepped in and helped them. I am not advocating that people who abused children are right for their behaviors; I am instead strongly encouraging healing through mindset change and forgiveness. It is hard to be angry with someone who you are viewing the same way you see yourself-- a child of God who was born pure and was victimized. I knew that I had to forgive the people they were when they were pure and free of the wrong, they did. I would have to forgive the person who was acting out what they learned. I would have to forgive a person I had not met.

This could potentially cause a debate since it took me awhile to come to this understanding. Just remember that everybody's journey of healing is different. I learned to filter the things that didn't work for me. I encourage everyone to do the same. In order to heal you must do what feels right. What gives you the best experience? What clears the knot from your gut? What allows you to not only survive, but live? I would encourage these beautiful souls to look pass their abuse and work on their healing. They would ask me how? I would say start with the hardest part. Forgiveness!

Speak It

I was not going to be defined by my sexual abuse. There is no time limit on when a person can speak their truth. Some people's first response is to say, "why are they just speaking up?" The hardest part of living your truth is sharing it for the first time. The reasons I was told why many people stayed silent was because of family, guilt, and believing they would get in trouble. These reasons and others were why I stayed silent for many years. When I got older it was more about not wanting to be judged or put in a box as a victim. But I quickly realized how freeing speaking my truth was. Once I started speaking it, I couldn't stop. Every time I shared, I felt lighter, like a weight of years of eating bad food was shedding. It was the poison to my soul that I just didn't want to keep anymore. I found the antidote. I found the cure, and the good news was it could cure others. Other women and men needed me to shout out and help them to free their cluttered minds. Too often I would have conversations with people and the signs of sexual abuse would be present, and I would open a dialog just to find out that we shared a common bond of darkness.

Part 2

Bonds of Healing

Bonds We Created

"There is a light in this world, a healing spirit more powerful than any darkness we may encounter." Mother Teresa

It was through my support of others that I felt the healing power. One of the things that I know for sure is that putting the pieces together does not happen overnight. It is a process, a journey, that will take you through many mountains and valleys. Throughout my process, I found that I was not alone in this search of the missing pieces in my life. There are so many women and men, girls and boys that I met with stories like mine, and sometimes worse. There is a silent bond that's formed when I meet someone who has been sexually abused. Someone usually shares a part of their story with a caution of what will the other person think about me. Often a bond is formed when trust is formed, and only then does the other person decide to share his or her story.

Way before the public #MeToo movement, people were bonding privately in search of healing. The #MeToo brought out to light the enormity of the issue of sexual abuse. It showed the world that sexual abuse does not discriminate by race, color, gender or economic status. It was quite empowering especially for those people who felt alone, and afraid to share. I personally congratulated and thanked many social media friends who joined the movement and made their stories known. They were respected professionals, mentors, teachers; but we all shared a common bond of silence, guilt, and shame. At some point we were seeking a way to make sense of it all. Now we could share without reservations. Now we saw others who we would have never imagined breaking the silence. We thought we were alone in the quest for healing.

I once read that the heart and hands are connected and after writing my stories, I realized how true that was for me. There are many ways to reach out and help others heal, however, I wanted to give them an outlet to let it out without judgment while helping others. Adding their stories in the *Bond of Healing* section of the book would be their medium. As I was encouraging a young lady to use this opportunity of writing her story, as a path to healing, I felt empowered. I felt as if I was at the right place at the right time. She needed to have the conversation because she said "It's making me want to cry. I wish I had someone to talk to when I was going through my abuse." I explained to her that the journey we take is like having a hole in our heart and each time we speak out, each time we bond with another survivor, we fill in a spot. We are mending our broken hearts. I started picturing a heart drawn on the piece of paper and me with a red crayon filling in the holes. I wanted to reach as many broken hearts and help them color in the empty spaces.

I will share some stories from women and men, with hopes that if you are reading this book you can find a story that resonates with you. These are stories that were shared with me and helped me in my journey and healing process. This is not a process that can be done alone. Not being able to talk about it allowed the negative emotions of guilt, shame, and doubt to take over. My bond of healing went beyond just women who had experienced sexual abuse--it extended to the men who cried in privacy.

I worked as a manager for many years, and during this time I met and counseled many women for different reasons. But what stood out were the stories they shared of abuse. Some of these women were mothers sharing stories of their husbands or significant others violating their daughters. Then there were the stories of women who managed to survive giving birth and raising a child that was born out of sexual abuse. And the hardest ones for me to grasp were the ones where the mothers turned a blind eye to the abuses that were being done to their daughters because they needed financial support.

Some were mothers that did not believe their daughter's cry for help because having a man in their own lives was far more important. I write for my sister friend who found out that her father, the man she loved so deeply, her "daddy," had sexually molested her sister. And what about the young girl I met at nineteen years old who became my little sister and was just comfortable enough nineteen years later to share her full story of abuse.

And then, there were the men who shared their stories with me. The one brother who was devastated by the news that his father, the man he idolized, had sexually abused his sisters. And what about the man who shared with me that he was sexually abused by his female babysitter. It was during this time in my life that I knew God had a purpose for me. I knew then, and I am sure now that my life, my story, my pain was not in vain. I started feeling that the only way I would be able to help others through their journey was to have experienced and lived it. It was with this realization that I stopped questioning *why?*

As I was preparing to write this section of my book, I started reaching out to some of the women and men who had shared their stories with me in the past. One sweet friend told me that she was happily married and saw no reason to revisit that situation. It's important to know that your journey is just that, yours. You should not force others to join you. Everyone has their time and calling. However, there were others that accepted the challenge before I could even ask them the question.

I will call this lady Tahlia. When I reached out to her, I wasn't certain that she would say yes, but I remembered her story, and I remembered her pain.

It started with a simple "Good Morning" through instant messaging where I said "Hi, it's been a long time. Do you mind if I call you? Are you available?" She responded right away, "Yes you can call me", and provided her number. That conversation lasted for one hour on that divine Sunday morning. As I described my book, and my intentions, she said, "I am excited already." I hadn't even told Tahlia what I needed from her, yet her excitement was coming through the phone. When I shared that I would be honored to have her share her story in a part of my book, she cried, and a deeper bond was formed. I knew then that I had chosen the right person, who through our hour-long conversation showed a vision that was aligned with mine.

Tahlia's Story

An abused child is a damaged child

As far back as I can remember was the age of five years old. Our neighbor next door was so infatuated with me she wanted to be the one to raise me. On day my mom packed my clothes and took me to her house. Back then I didn't understand why my mom only let me go to live with this neighbor out of five of her daughters, but later in life it became clear to me. The neighbor's name was Annette, and she was raising three young boys of her own. She was so nice to me--she would dress me up in nice dresses, do my hair in pretty ponytails and put on little hats to match my dresses. Growing up I was always an attention seeker (look at me, look at me), showing off something or another. Little did I know it would lead me into some real dark places in my life.

I lived with Annette for over a year and her two older sons treated me as a sister. They played with me and took care of me while she was gone. However, the younger son would play with my private areas while we were supposed to be taking a nap. Because I was so young, I didn't know if that was appropriate, so I never told a soul. I was scared and ashamed. It went on for months with me not saying a word, then one day my dad came to the house and said he was moving the entire family to South Carolina and was taking his baby girl with him. I was so happy to be back with my family and even more happy not have to be scared or ashamed anymore.

Once we moved from Alabama to South Carolina things were not as I expected it to be. The year apart from my sisters made a huge difference. I was the middle child, so the two older sisters and two younger sisters had formed a bond between each other that did not include me. Most of my time was spent following behind my daddy doing his paper route or under the cars working with him, or just generally getting in the way. My bond with my mother was never close. As a child I could never remember her telling me she loved me or hugging me. Because I was that attention seeker, I really needed that and when I didn't get it, I would act out in school. There were times I would throw desks in class and fight whomever stood in my way. My anger was uncontrollable. Once my behavior became uncontrollable, I felt my mother gave up on me and only tolerated it because she had to. This behavior continued until my early twenties. Then it would turn in to depression most of the time.

When I was twelve years old my parents divorced, and I stayed in the house with my four sisters and mother. I was so miserable. I missed my dad so much. I started getting into even more trouble and even took pills to try to end my life. The attention I got from my dad was no longer in our house and even though I saw him some weekends, it was not enough.

When I was fourteen my mom got remarried and he seemed like a nice guy. I was excited about having a father like my dad in the house. He played with us, hugged us, and showed lots of love. Then one day I was riding alone with him and he said he needed to stop by his old house. When we got there, I was hesitating, but he said, "Come on in," so I did. When we got in, he took my hand and lead to a bedroom. He started touching on me, and even though I said stop it didn't matter--he continued. I didn't know what else to do, so I just laid there. When it was over, he told me not to tell anyone. I didn't think anybody would believe me anyway because I was such a troubled child.

This continued for months until I had a very angry outburst and ran away to my dad's house. I was dating a young guy and told him what my stepdad had been doing to me, and he told my father. My father called my mom and she said I was a "liar." A few hours later she threw all my clothes on the lawn and said I was not welcome in her home anymore.

I lived with my dad for a few years until we were evicted because my dad was an alcoholic and wasn't paying the bills. I began living with aunts, friends, strangers, and even slept in cars. Despite being homeless for a year, I managed to continue going to school. It wasn't until a janitor found out I was homeless and informed the authorities that it was addressed. I then began living in foster homes. From the age of sixteen to eighteen I went to five different high schools and four foster families.

I became pregnant with my son at seventeen and had him when I was eighteen, all while going to school and working. Once I graduated, I had saved enough money to get my own car and apartment. Two years later I had my daughter and was still estranged from my mother and all my sisters.

When the truth came out about my stepfather, my sisters and mother called me a "liar" and said I just like to make trouble like I always did.

Molesters always know who to target because of the victim's personality and how well the family shows support to that person. Well, me being a "liar" all changed when I was around twenty-one years old. I was living alone with my two children and got a call at 5am from one of my sisters whom I had not spoken to in years. She had to be around seventeen years old. She was crying and said she woke up to our stepfather in her bed. Months later another sister said he was on the floor looking under the bathroom door at her. Things got a little more serious now that they knew I wasn't lying. However, this did not stop my mom from staying married to him or my sisters from being around him. After time went on, they all forgot about it and forgave him, and I was still hurting. I was hurting more from the neglect of my sisters and especially my mom, the person that was supposed to protect us all.

As time went on, I lost contact with them and continued my life as a single mom. During this time, I figured out a lot about myself. I was in such a dark spot I still had that anger I had as a child and I took it out on my children. By the time I was in my late twenties I noticed my moods would change often and I couldn't figure out why. I knew the molestation had to have something to do with it, so I went to the alter at church one day and asked God to help me forgive my abuser and my mom so that I could move on with my life. Hoping it would remove the mood swings, anxiety and depression, I continued to pray on it until I saw a change. I started being more successful in my career and could afford to quit my second job, but my mood and depression were still there. This lasted up until I met the man of my dreams.

I always hid my mood swings and depression to the outside world; only my children knew about it and were not sure what was happening to their mother. We just went with it and prayed I would get normal. But once I met this man it could not be our family secret anymore because he wanted to marry me. He convinced me to see a therapist and I was diagnosed with Bipolar disorder.

Once I researched what Bipolar was and how it affected me it changed my life. It also opened my eyes to so many events in my childhood and adult life.

I am now on the right medications that minimize my mood swings and depression. I am now married with a beautiful home, a great career, and have opened my very own Eyelash Bar. But most importantly, I have forgiven my mom and we have since fostered a good relationship, something I craved during my younger years. Praise My God!

When my dear friend shared this story many years ago, we were in a work environment, and she was only able to tell the story at the surface. However, recently when I met her at her beautiful home for breakfast, we ate, shared stories, we laughed together, and we cried a lot. It was evident that there was love in her home. She finally had created the environment she always wanted as a child. She was determined to shine in her career, her business, and especially her marriage since she found a man who also adored her. There is a beacon of light that comes from my dear friend. She exudes honesty, openness, and a willingness to help others around her. We talked about not being defined by our sexual abuse, and her getting the help she needs to stay balanced. I declare that with all she has been through, to be able to still have such love for her mother, who is still married to her abuser, she is the epitome of a true survivor.

John's Story

The Gut Shot

I met a friendly and nice man while I was at gymnastics with my daughter. He was full of life and always came to the gym with his beautiful girls in tow. We immediately hit it off since we were both talkers. The conversation that led us to him sharing his story was a simple one. We were talking about our children, and I told him that I am a protective and aware mother to my children especially my daughter. I told him I would give up the world just to keep her safe. He asked me, "Why is that?" The rest was the creation of a beautiful friendship, as he shared his pain and fears for his children. He called it "the gut shot."

> Disbelief, numbness, nausea and devastation. Just a few feelings that infiltrated my body as this little nugget of information shot through my soul. A myriad of questions swirled. *Did he admit to this?*

Or were these merely unfounded accusations? All my sisters? No way! Not my dad! The desire to process this information instantly burned.

When I discovered that my dad had sexually abused two of my sisters, I was thirty-four years old and married with three daughters. The news did not come from one of my six siblings. Instead it was passed along in conversation to my wife. I was the only sibling that was devoid of this devastating news. Why was I the last to know is still a mystery.

After giving myself a few days to process this life changing news, I had to face reality and call my mom. It just so happened it was her birthday. As we spoke of what I had learned, I could hear her responded as if the life got sucked out of her. I knew the truth about her husband. Her focus immediately went into damage control. She seemed eager to know who had told me. She then shifted into defending him. I was stunned! It was almost as if she was upset at me for knowing. I then had to endure a speech about how he had changed and how great of a father he was to me. I didn't want to hear any of it. A couple of thoughts clouded me as I spoke with her.

The first thought was how and why no one told me earlier. I had three daughters for Christ sake! This man was alone with them on several occasions. There was no reason for withholding this information. How can anyone ever excuse such negligence?

Second, how did my mother come to the decision to stay with this man after discovering he violated her daughters' innocence and self-worth?

Wasn't her number one priority as a parent to protect her children? She did not fulfill this duty. In my mind the only viable next step should have been for her to distance herself from this man. But she failed!

Many months after the initial conversation, I spoke with my mom again to get a better understanding of what happened. She said one of the reasons she stayed was for financial security for the family. She explained that we would have been homeless had she left. She also gave him a chance with a therapist to "fix himself." Apparently after a few sessions, he was deemed "cured" and wouldn't repeat the behavior. I was speechless! I wasn't buying either reason. I tried effortlessly not to judge her decision, but as a father myself, I was not successful.

As I worked through this turmoil in my mind, I also had to figure out how my wife and I were going to move forward with our relationship with my parents. At that time, they were still married. They have since divorced after forty-nine years of marriage. My wife and

I had countless discussions about how and if we would forge a relationship with them. My brothers and sisters found a way to form some semblance of a relationship, but they had years to process the information and figure it out. We certainly could not trust my father to be around our daughters alone. Without trust, a relationship cannot prosper. Especially knowing the horrible things he had done to his own daughters.

During these times I faced many challenges, one of them was trying to decipher a nagging memory or nightmare I carried with me for as long as I could remember. In this memory, I was molested by a member of my family. I am certain is was not my father but could not figure out who it might have been. I thought these memories were merely a result of my nightmares, until I learned of my father's horrific actions. Now I believe it was real.

I shared this belief with my older sister and she faintly remembers something similar happening to her. Her memory of any sexual abuse at the hands of my father is also cloudy, but she believes something happened. We even agreed that it was our older sister that violated us. I have yet to confront her about this possibility. Unearthing this truth requires a stable mind and superior coping skills, both of which I do not possess.

Processing all of this has been a challenge both physically and mentally. I have yet to conquer the demons I still carry from my time in Iraq as a soldier. As I write this, I still haven't completely processed any of this in a healthy manner. Controlling my anger has become a challenge. Trust in others has vanished. I am aware that I cannot let this fester inside me because no one wins with that method. Fast forward six years after the truth reared its ugly head, and my wife and I added two more daughters to our squad. I have realized now why I was blessed with five lovely daughters. My role as their father is to show them how a father is supposed to treat his daughters. Although my own dad was unable to teach me how to be a strong and decent father and husband, he taught me what not to be. Therein lies the silver lining. Sadly, some of our most profound lessons derive from mistakes within our personal circle. Unfortunately, my own father's mistakes have provided me the opportunity to be a better man than he ever could be. For that, I am grateful.

After he wrote this, he shared with me that he still had a lot of anger inside him that needs to be addressed. He said that he was relieved when I shared my story with him. "Your willingness to expose the truth and be vulnerable is both courageous and therapeutic. You are a true example of light and hope".

But my friend had to understand that

vulnerability was a necessary part of my healing process.

Blake's Story

Alone in the Crowd

I had a moment to bond with Blake and what we realized was how much our lives were parallel. Our conversation started out with laughs as we talked about how I asked my angels to help me find a pair of gold shoes to wear to my cousin's wedding. "I ask my angels for help with everything, even to help me buy shoes." We laughed out loud as I gave him several fun examples, and then he reverently said, "you have faith." I knew the conversation was going to get heavy; I knew laughter would turn into tears.

It wasn't just the fact that he was sexually abused by our family member. He suffered more from abandonment that he believes opened the door for the abuse. "I had no one," he said to me. "I was alone in a crowd of people and no one knew I was there." His words were filled with pain and regret, yet his soul was overrun with kindness and humility. It was an odd combination, especially for someone who had been through so much hurt and pain. As he explained about the days when he would run and hide from his own family, my heart ached as tears fell from both of our eyes. I tried to be strong for him, to let him know it will be fine. But even I, the ultimate optimist, had doubt. How will he ever live a "normal" life after all that? I looked at him and I said, "you are broken on the inside, but I will be there for you to help pick up the pieces." I knew it was going to be a challenging task because he had carried this pain for over thirty years.

As he reminisced about when his mother left him and his brothers, he was not even a year old. She left as so many had done before her. To find a "better life" for her and her children. His formative years were spent without the nurturing hands, and kind words of a mother. He was left in a household filled with people who all had their own life agendas and truly had no time for an extra child. As we talked, we resolved it by saying, "There were so many of us." It's amazing that even with how much we have been through, we always try to find a way to let people off the hook. He held back a lot of the details of the abuse because he said when he speaks it, he relives it through nightmares and depression. He explained that there was a loose floorboard under a bed in our grandparent's room that he would lift and climb through to the bottom of the house to hide. "Everyone thought I was weird, but I was just hiding." He hid in the cages with the chickens, he hid under beds, and he hid in barrels. He was being tormented in his own house by his own family, and no one helped him.

He said one day he thought he was saved. His father came to pick him up; he told him to pack his bags and come. As he explained his heightened sense of relief and excitement that his abuse would be over, it was crushed. He explained that our grandmother said he could not go, and when his father insisted, his abuser threatened his father and he did not get the freedom that he had longed for.

"I just wanted someone to ask me, I would have told if I was asked." The truth is no one was paying attention, or if they were, the dirty secrets were kept in order to avoid the trepidations, and consequences that would follow. He said his grandmother took him to church with her a lot. Not just on Sundays, but every time she would go. Women's meeting, prayer meetings, Bible studies, Sunday school, and regular services. He said he did not understand why she took him away from the house so much and one day he said to her "I want to go to hell." He said she explained that she just wanted him to know God. It was at that moment we both had an epiphany and we said, she was handling it the best way she knew how. He agreed and shared that now he is grateful that she took him to church because it laid a biblical and spiritual foundation that helped him to smile through the pain, cry in private, and restrain the anger and rage that were brewing within.

He had gone through a lot more as he spent many days locked up in local jails because someone stole his identity. He said he was convinced he was cursed, "Why me?" He said, "I didn't even cry while I was locked up." He was amazed by where he found the strength. But as we spoke, we both knew that the spiritual foundation that was forced on him had saved his life. We both knew that he knew God. It was apparent to us that our grandmother had a clue. He said it was during his time locked up that he re-discovered the God he had spent all those hours as a young boy getting to know.

I just wanted to hug him and not let go. I wanted to make it go away with love, but it wasn't that simple. His deep-rooted issue continued past his abuse. He said his mother came to visit and one of our aunts insensitively lined up all the boys and asked his mother to pick her children out of the line-up. Of course, after being gone for so many years she did not recognize him. She did not pick her own son.

He explained how devastated he was as he ran off. As the saying goes "salt was added to the wound." We grew up in a culture where many women and men left their children to be raised with relatives in search of something better. I am sure that not every situation led to abuse, but the cases are staggering. What they didn't know was when they left, it was a breeding ground for abuse and neglect. Every child needs their own advocate, and who is a better candidate then their actual parents.

The abuse didn't stop when he finally got the escape he had longed for. His mother moved all her boys with her after thirteen years of separation, but the household she moved them to lacked love and was filled with physical and mental abuse. He said he had anger toward the family and the relationship he saw between his younger siblings and his mother. The love she gave them that he never got. He said it was just as hard living with his mother as it was living without her. It was just a different type of abuse. He became that person. "Hurt people, hurt people." Because of this he ruined relationships that he believes are now irreparable. He lacked stability as he moved from house to house to seek out a sense of nurturing and love. He said he found it with one aunt who treated him with kindness. He holds her in high regards because she gave him what he longed for.

Why didn't you tell someone? As I asked that question, I felt like a hypocrite, because I didn't tell anyone when my abuse was happening, and I believed I knew his answer. But I really didn't. He said his abuser said he would kill him if he told anyone. Then as he got older, he was afraid to tell because he knew in his heart that someone would seriously hurt or kill his abuser based on the culture we lived in. He was stuck between a rock and a hard place. He was in a classic victim role, where he started rationalizing the outcome to find a good one. There is usually no good outcome.

He went on to say that he was going to keep it a secret because all he wanted was to pretend it didn't happen. After he got married and had a child, he just wanted to provide the life he never had. He said his wife was a better mother to his daughter than the mother he had, and he was going to be a better father than his father was to him. He had a plan to move on without addressing his past. He was going to continue to pretend that it didn't happen. But one day he was confronted with the question and he told the truth. As he said, "I just wanted someone to ask me."

The enormity of this situation is felt now as an adult. It is deeper than any of us could ever imagine. The pain and hurt that I felt as he told his story and only the surface because the deeper he went the harder it was. Why relive it? Why bring it all up and cripple his mind and body all over again? Because only through that pain will he get the healing he needs. One of the worse parts of his story was being victimized over again when he was asked as an adult to not say anything in order to spare the reputation of his abuser. To that I said, "He had no right to ask you to do that." I explained the great need for him to get professional help, as it was clear to me that he has a job that was bigger than himself. "One step at time," I told him, "but you will help many others during your journey of healing."

On that night as I talked with Blake and cried with him about something so deep and so destructive, I wondered if

I had failed him. Was there something I could have done? It's amazing how the aftermath of abuse have us wondering what we could have done. That night I learned a lesson that I will carry with me for the rest of my life. He said he wished he knew he had me to talk to all these years as he carried the secret and the feeling of abandonment and rage within his heart. He thought I had it together and everything was "perfect." He thought there was no way I would understand him. It was through those words that I realized how much transparency can help others. However, my transparency and vulnerability came with maturity.

George's Story

Hard work hides the Pain

It started as an innocent game of hide and seek between two young friends. They were only nine years old and that's one of the harmless games that children play. Yet as they played, someone had a baleful thought for these boys. He said this man, the next-door neighbor decided he wanted to play hide and seek with the them. He thought it was a bit strange since he was a grown-up but kept gleefully playing as children do. He said it was during this game that it all went wrong. "He used to always try to touch us and say things to us, me and my best friend". This is what George shared about one of his abusers. George remembers the room he was hiding, but he is missing most of the details. He said his memory is blurred, and there is a part of his life that seems to be missing. "I don't remember much from age five to fourteen. I just want to curl up and cry myself back to five years old". I am not a doctor, but it seemed to me that period of his life must have had some traumatic incidents and his mind has decided to tuck it away.

As I encouraged George to release the poison from his body by speaking his truth, he struggled. He wanted to let it out but said he did not know how to put it in words. I encouraged him by reminding him I was here to help him heal and there will be no judgment. I told him his words did not have to be perfection, or pretty, just let them out. As he vented the poison from his soul, he was able to share his feelings better with words as he cried. "I am so hurt! I just want to run! Run just run!" To this I responded, "I understand but we can't run from ourselves."

George wrote in his text that it was not only the incident with the male neighbor, but there were a few women who were neighbors that would "mess with us" every time they came to the house. George's use of "us" made me cringe, because that meant there were others who these women traumatized. George explained that two of these women moved into the neighborhood after a major hurricane hit, and the other was the girlfriend of one of his relatives. This was a good reminder that sexual abuse does not discriminate. The offenders are both men and women, and the victims are boy and girls.

George continued to say, "I love my family, but I expected more protection from them, but what do you do? I just want to be free" He explained that he buried his pain in his work and has always done that since he was a little boy. He said he had many responsibilities as a boy, and he wondered how he handled them and school without falling apart. He was responsible for taking care of the dogs, he cooked for the entire family, and still did great in school.

The part of his story that stirred the most emotion was not what happened to him, but what he witnessed. He shared that one day he saw one of his relatives walking away from a crying Blake. He said when the relative saw him he threatened to throw him in the gully when it rained so that he would wash away. He said that incident traumatized him for a lifetime as he suffers with fear of going into the ocean, pool, or any body of water. He also expressed some guilt from not sharing what he thought he saw on that day. "I thought he had given him a whipping since he was always beating on us". I understood his guilt and it made me sad. Since we are often taught to be our brother's keeper it has devastated him to learn the truth about Blake was what he witnessed that day.

As George tried to forge a different life for himself and his family, the darkness from his past continues to erode his mind and block him from living. He has been merely surviving all these years. He still works long hours and play the fixer role to everyone as if he is trying to make amends for not speaking up over thirty years ago. He shared with me that the intro music to one of his favorite television shows causes him deep sadness and put him in a place back to his childhood every time he hears it. "I am just standing there on the bridge and I am sad. I don't see anything or anyone, just me on the bridge." The song takes him to a familiar place with a familiar emotion, but no clarity of why. The eerie part of this story is that when I listened to the words associated to the song, they had a strange correlation to his life. But George had never listened to the words of the song.

I told him to believe that every step of his journey, the chaos, the betrayals, the lies, and the hurt was designed to be a part of his healing. I cried as I imagined the guilt he must be carrying, along with the confusion of the cloudy gap in memory from his young life. I encouraged him to continue down the path of healing as it will afford him the freedom of the mind that he has longed for.

If this was a handwritten copy and you were reading the original manuscript of my book, you would bear witness to the water marks made from the tears I cried as I wrote my story, and the stories of those I bonded with. But George's story was a hard one for me. It became personal, it resonated on so many levels that there were times it took away my breath. George was the second generation of who endured this harrowing experience and one of the males who were brave enough to speak their truth. His mother was a survivor of sexual abuse and emotional neglect. When she left her children behind, she did not know she was leaving them in the "lion's den." She was told that they would be taken care of. She was told to go and make life better for them. When you grow up without money and you think that is the path to stability, then you do things like leave your children behind in search of that financial security. But when she left the situation for her children became dire. Her departure would change their lives and her bond with them forever.

When she left, she barely understood herself since she had been a victim trapped in the web of secrecy. She lived in a space where there was a lack of compassion and there was merely a life of survival. She left without a thought that something so devastating would happen to her boys, since she had only known it to happen to the girls.
Imagine that feeling for a mother when she discovered that her sons were violated and left with lifetime wounds and emotional

battle scars. By the time they were reunited it was too late and the gray skies had turn black. They were hurt and resentful.

Stories like this are what motivate me to say no more. It's because of stories like this that we must share and break the cycle. George was the age that my beautiful daughter is now, and where my son once was. When I think of his experience, I was sick. But this kind, hardworking, beautiful soul that I know him to be made his story almost unbearable.

I applauded George for speaking his truth and offering his story with hopes that it will help others. I encouraged him to start the healing journey and face his fears so that he can be whole again. We talked about knowing his reason and purpose. It's his family, his children that give him his will to keep going. Although he experienced such betrayal from some of his family members, he still expressed deep and sincere love for them. I encouraged professional help, because sometimes our story is so deep that we need God and a doctor. This was a tough one.

I imagine doing a family tree and next to each name I put a symbol for which of them were sexually abused as a child. The visual I had was alarming, and disturbing. Throughout my journey of writing this book, I found a correlation between abandonment and child molestation at an alarming rate. The lack of support and protection made us easy targets. Therefore, I professed that if you put your child in my hands, I would treat him/her like the delicate gem that they are. This is because I once wished I was treated like a pearl.

Letter to Blake and George

A Mother's Plea

My Dear Sons

I am writing you this letter asking, no begging for your forgiveness. Please forgive me for leaving you in such a hostile environment. My life was never an easy one. From the age of seven I was sexually molested by the neighbor. I told mom and she shooed me away. I screamed it! I yelled it! No one believed me and it happened repeatedly by different people. I was told to "shut up" and that I "complained too much"

One of my brothers physically abuse me

and another sexually abused me and yet my mother turned a blind eye to it all. Then my cousin raped me while I was knocked out on medicine and I got pregnant. When I told my truth, I was told I was lying, and it became a lifelong story for everyone else who was not living my truth. During my pregnancy I hid under the bed, in the wardrobe and only went out to the doctors. During this time, I attempted several suicide attempts.

I tried to be good all my life and could not understand why things were not going the way I intended it to go. The plan for my life was to finish my nursing and get married and leave home. The person I was going to marry was pressuring me to be intimate and I did not want that so when I ended up pregnant for someone else, he was angry. I made plans to meet him and explain the situation about the pregnancy and it ended up as another forced sex situation. I always try to be good and do good, yet my life was one disaster after another.

I had a good friend whose son I was taking care of, and when I told him I was pregnant with my second child, he said, "let me be the father" I said "I can't do that" and he said he was going to tell everyone that he was the father. That started a rumor, but the truth is between me and God. This friend even went to my mother to ask permission to marry me and she told him he was not good enough for me and did everything within her power to chase him away. I was determined to leave home and thought if I got pregnant again with my third, she would let me go, but that didn't work.

So, I did what I had to do to support myself and you boys. I raised chickens, goats, sold eggs, peanuts, Irish moss, roots, I sewed and did childcare. I was doing well financially; but I was still being abused physically by my brother and I was not happy living there. I knew my mom was not the warm and fuzzy type, but I notice that she really loved her grandchildren.

There were a set of unfortunate

circumstances that led to my departure from Jamaica. I was asked to taking care of my cousins' children who had brought them from Canada, and when it was time for them to go home, I was asked to take them back. The arrangements were made, the ticket was bought, I got a visa for a three-month visit. Before I left Jamaica, your aunt and I had an agreement to take charge of your care while I was gone. I left your bank accounts with her in charge, and she promised me she would take care of you boys like you were her own. I wholeheartedly believed that she would. It was not easy for me to leave, but I believed this trip would make a way for a better life for us.

I was only in Canada for two weeks when I realized things were not right. My cousin disappeared with my passport and left me stranded in a bus station where I knew no one and most people spoke French. My three-month visit to Canada turned into a nightmare. I was plagued with the guilt of leaving you behind. I endured threats and extortion from my own sister and there was a constant need to send money home to make sure you boys where cared for. It never crossed my mind that my boys would be sexually abused. It was painful knowing I was sending money and you were just a piggy bank, but the pain of knowing you were sexually violated is unexplainable.

I ask God for forgiveness daily, but I do hope one day you my sons can find it in their hearts to forgive me. Please Forgive Me!

Laura's Story

Family Affair

It was a beautiful fall Sunday morning, and I was driven to make the phone call. The day before I had reached out to Blake and we talked about his story and how it made him feel. As we were talking, and I was working on making sure he understood how important it was that he spoke up and that he should not feel guilty for speaking the truth, I shared a piece of my story. When I shared about my aunt's boyfriend who violated me as a young girl, he mentioned our other relative who was a survivor at the hands of the same person. I knew within that moment that my work was so much bigger than myself.

The next day I sent a message to her that simply said "Call me." She called me right away and the bond of healing began. I didn't do any small talk, because this was a relative that I had spent a lot of time with when I was in my twenties. I served as a big sister, we spent time talking about her dreams, goals and aspirations. I adored her daughter and welcomed their company. I always knew her spirit was broken, but I did not know her story, only in my dreams. But within this moment I was able to share with her the dark bond we shared at the hands of the same person. We cried together, and I encouraged her to speak up and never stop. I apologized to her for abandoning her but explained that it was not because I didn't love her, or that I felt like I was "better than." I walked away from family to dig deeper into my healing process, since I was unable to do so with the many reminders around.

I shared stories of how I went about my healing. I explained to her that the process is life long, but it must be done to save at least one child. I asked about her daughter who I adored so much. Was she abused? Did he get to her? I released a sigh of relief when she said no, "I protected her by telling her to stay away from him, and by keeping her by my side." We talked about how she felt when she visited that "house" we grew up in. I shared that I understood why she did not like visiting. But I encouraged her of the importance of facing it head on so that she does not become our mothers, aunts, uncles, grandparents, who all suffocated their pain and hurt and left a cycle of sexual abuse to continue. I shared with her the importance of not caring if people believed her story, if she told it the way she remembered it. She then agreed to send me what she had been writing over the years. She would share her work of healing to help to save a life.

She told me that many years ago she told her truth to our grandmother, and it was passed on and eventually reached her mother. But the result was not one of healing for this young girl. Her mother threw a telephone and hit her and called her a "liar." But it wasn't until this conversation with Laura that I understood her mother was so devastated when I told her what her boyfriend did to me. Because she was not hearing this for the first time. Many years before me her own daughter shared the same story about the same man and only God knows who else. The sadness in this was that a cycle was not broken and even continued to another generation, because Laura had not learned how to break it. This was proven when I had a conversation with a much younger family member. The cycle continued because no one helped.

It was that moment when I cried silent tears and the thought in my head was "oh no, not you too". Because even with the #MeToo movement I wanted and prayed that there would be friends and family members that would truthfully say "Thank God, not me." But this one young girl had said "not me" before, but this time she had to speak her truth. Maybe it was the news of losing a peer to suicide that made her decide it was time to share her deepest secret. Or maybe it was the comforting words I spoke about wanting to make sure she was emotionally well. But she spoke it, and as much as I was glad that she was able to release that venom from her soul, my eyes cried because I wished it wasn't so. I recognized it in the lack of confidence in the way she smiled in her shy understated demeanor. Although her words said "no, not me", her eyes had a longing to share. We are still sitting on that information as if we are frozen in time. I know that I will have to address this in a way that no one addressed it with me. I will not turn a blind eye, or deaf ears. She spoke it, which was the hard part, now the healing will start with my support.

Kasha's Story

Quiet Storm

It was just amazing to me how many women I would talk to who either experienced sexual abuse in some form or another or were struggling with the guilt of not protecting their child. We can work hard at protecting our children by arming them with the truth and letting them know they can trust you to defend them. Build their confidence and always remind them that they have a voice. The things we cannot avoid are those moments when we get busy doing the everyday things we do as parents. We go to work, our children visit with friends, and we trust our spouse. My lovely coworker and I had a conversation years ago, and it was then I saw the hurt and pain she was going through. She shared it in what she called the "Quiet Storm."

> As a wife and mother of three children life was extremely busy, and most of the time there was hardly any time left for me. Dealing with daily life routines, work, and the pressures of taking care of a family can cause one to see only what's before them. And sometimes in these instances, so much can go unnoticed, unseen, and unfortunately unprotected.

I will never forget the night my life changed forever. The night that my husband, the man I married, the man I trusted and vowed to honor, came to me in tears, crying hysterically. His words will forever resonate in the corridor of my mind, "I molested my daughter." I thought I was clearly mistaken. There must be something wrong with my ears, but again he said, "I molested my daughter." Since we have three daughters, two of which are my husband's and then my eldest, his stepdaughter, I was uncertain as to which daughter he was referring. So, for a moment, I paused. I fought through the heat that rose over me and paused the welling tears in my eyes, and I calmly went to my eldest daughter. "Did he hurt you? Tell me the truth, and I promise that I will protect you."

There were several minutes of a black out, lost time within the moment. I do not remember some of what I said or parts of what I did. I do remember locking my daughter in her room and heading to the kitchen for a knife. This foul, evil, deplorable excuse of a man, deserved to pay. Then I thought to myself, who will protect my kids when they no longer have me? "Vengeance is mine, saith the Lord." This single thought calmed me, and I put the knife away and packed up my kids, and that very night we left.

No one ever thinks about how much it takes to refrain from hurting someone that you feel deserves pain. It took hours for me to come to myself enough to know that it was time to go into survival mode. I didn't have time to cry, whine, or break down. I had to be strong and be the woman of God and mother I know my children needed me to be.

After finding out that my

fourteen-year-old daughter had been molested since she was eleven years old and now was impregnated by my husband, to say that I felt like a failure was an understatement. I was hit by a quiet storm that did more damage than a category five hurricane. It felt like the damage was irreversible. I did not, would not, subject my daughter to the heckles of being a teenage mother with a pregnancy that was beyond her control, and the child was aborted. With very mixed emotions I might add.

After years of trying to put our lives back together, my

children and I stand triumphant and stronger than ever. We all struggled emotionally to get through this devastating time. We had to learn how to rely on each other and depend on those I knew would support us.

Unfortunately, this meant distancing my children from their paternal relatives. Tragedy will always show you who is really in your corner. This trauma that my girls and I were experiencing had my own family members doubting, judging, and blaming me. It was hard enough that I was experiencing my own guilt, but it was hurtful to think my own family thought I would intentionally let anyone hurt my children. I fought for my children because I felt that they were all I had, because they knew me better than anyone.

My ex-husband served ten years in prison for this crime. Even with him gone, I found it imperative to ask more questions, pay more attention, be more involved and not trust anyone to simply do the right thing. My family and I survived this quiet storm. Like a rattle snake, it struck in silence, and we were able to thrive in secret. But we are survivors and are victorious because of our faith in God, our love for one another, and the belief that forgiveness is the ultimate healer. Guilt will be forever with me. The guilt of not being able to protect my child was and will forever be something I battle, because that's what a mother is supposed to do--they protect. I thank God for the strength to forgive myself and that my daughter has also forgiven me. I rest in the fact that we made it together.

Her story had a similar ring to others I had heard. It also mimicked my own. It happened right there in her house by someone she loved and trusted. The turmoil that followed, the guilt, and the shame all helped to build the courage and strength of a mother and her three daughters.

Stephanie's Story

When It Happens to Your Mother

Sometimes your truth is not what happened to you, but what you witnessed. She was only a young girl of thirteen years old when she got to witness what became a traumatic, and lifetime battle for her. She said she can still hear the sounds, she remembers the words, and she saw it all from her hiding place. When we talked about it, I could feel her pain. I remember how awful it felt for me when I heard this story, that the house was broken into at gun point and her mother was sexually assaulted. I tried not to think about it. But how heart wrenching it was to hear the story from one of the victims. No, she was not a rape victim, but she had to bear witness to her mother being raped, while she stayed still to go undetected. She doesn't speak about it often, and never got help for this thirty-year tragedy. But the last time we saw each other I encouraged her to reach through the pain to find her healing. She shared that she struggled with her relationships with men because of trust issues created by that dark day. The hardest part for her was how it was handled by her mother the next day. She said her mother never discussed it with her and kept it moving like it never happened. She said all she wanted to do was talk about it with her mother.

Although the sexual abuse was not inflicted on her body, she had to watch it happen to her mother and I can only imagine how confused she was as a young girl. What I know for sure is that incident along with the physical abuse she endured from another relative has changed her forever. On that day, as we laid next to each other pouring out our hearts until three am, she talked about how she works hard to protect her children. She created a home where her children know they are loved, but with strong discipline. Her boys view her as the "stalker mom" who needs to know their every move. We laughed about it, but I saw her as loving mother working hard to break the cycle and keep her children safe. It made me proud. Just like you never stop learning, you never stop healing. Healing is a lifelong process that continues until you die.

Amelia's Story

Never Too Soon

There was a seventeen-year-old young lady with whom I spoke who made me ponder this question--is there an age that is too young to start your healing journey? I was informally counseling her about starting her healing journey, since she had already recognized that she had a story. Her anger, hurt, and disappointment didn't need to marinate into a pickle before she started to address it. "Use it to help," others I said. But as much as this seventeen-year-old was an old soul and wise beyond her years, she reminded me of her age by stating, "I am not ready."

Of course, she was not ready! That would mean being vulnerable and the V word is not an easy thing, especially when your foundation of trust is shaky. Trust is something that is built from the womb. And when you are born in a situation less than your choosing, such as this young lady was, then trust becomes a missing link. The people who were chosen to help this young lady to rebuild continued to break her. Not in the same ways her undesirable parents did, or the ways her abusers did, but they broke her just the same by failing to build that trust she longed for. They drove a wedge through the already shattered pieces--one knowingly and the other was just an act of God.
As we messaged that day about how she

wanted to be a motivational speaker, I knew then that if she already had that goal, she had a story. I told her that it would be great if other young people her age could hear her story. It was then that I thought *what if we could get our young people the support they needed at an age that would help them avoid the avalanche of issues that would later compound and fester into a larger wound? How great would it be if we could help stop the ripples? But since our hurt comes in stages, then that wouldn't solve them all. Or could it?* It was in this moment that I wondered—how might her life be different than my own if she could at the young age of seventeen nip the blighted growth now. The abandonment issues, the physical abuse, the mental abuse, the neglect, the sexual abuse, the mommy issues, the daddy issues— could we save this human being from a lifetime of headaches?

I watched a Ted Talk about the impact of childhood trauma on your health, and it made me realize that the earlier these issues are addressed the better for this young lady. It may seem like the easier road is to stay in avoidance. Although avoidance can be a cool place, because you don't have to face the music, it won't be long before your truth rears its head. I will continue to encourage and guide this young lady to start her healing journey now, as it could be a matter of living a healthier life.

Cara's Story

Strange Bond

To judge another is to inflict judgment on yourself. The reason I believe that strongly is because of Cara. I truly bonded with my Cara years after we met. She had decided to move away and left her children behind. I was confused and shocked that a "healthy" woman who seemed to love her children could just leave them. For a moment I judged her. I know how I felt about my children and I couldn't imagine leaving them behind willingly. And so, I judged. But one day while her daughter was visiting with me, we called her so that she could have some face time. The mother who answered the phone was not one who didn't want to be around her children. It was a woman who was scared. I couldn't help myself and I shared with Cara that I was judging her, and I needed to understand why she left her children behind. It was on that day that I learned her truth as follows:

> "I don't want to hurt them or have them witness me hurting anyone. I grew up with a mentally sick father and a codependent mother. She allowed so much to go on and always took his side because she feared losing his affections. I

feel safer with distance. I have been trying to kill myself since I was twelve years old. When I was younger, it was because I didn't feel like I belonged on earth or in the home I grew up in. My father had a way of making me feel like I was nothing and a horrible person. When I was my daughter's age, I was under so much stress at home and school. I was being molested by a cousin, bullied at school for being black, and dealing with all sorts of perverse sexual rumors while maintaining honor roll. I carried all that around until it started to impact my grades. At fifteen years old I was diagnosed with depression. I felt so alone. I would just take pills and hope to never wake up. By the time I was eighteen I was raped, and I never told anyone until I met my husband several years later. When I was raped, I reached out to my parents and asked for a counselor, they told me no one had time to take me. I wanted to quit school and they wouldn't let me. I stayed until I couldn't anymore, and then I started stripping. The day after September 11, after the towers got hit, I checked myself into the mental hospital. All of this happened to me before I was twenty-one years old.

Like I said, before you cast judgment on others look in the mirror. Cara wrote a book of poems, expressing the hurt for herself and her oldest daughter who she was unable to protect from the vicious cycle. Because no one helped her with her healing as a child she felt that she was not equipped to provide nurturing and support to her girls.

When Cara went away, she was starting her healing journey. She had gotten herself trapped in a cycle she learned as a child. She was living in an unhealthy marriage and struggled to break herself free. Although she loved her girls, she didn't feel like she had what it took to be a good mother to them. No one showed her how to do it, and she was repeating a destructive cycle. So, Cara felt that leaving was best for her. When she left, she went to a different country, new culture, new people, with a new lifestyle. She was running in order to discover herself.

It was six months after she shared her truth she moved back and rejoined her children, and her true healing began. She is no longer in an unhealthy marriage and can now recognize the dysfunction that she tolerated for so many years. She knows that it will be challenging with many hills and valleys. However, she is showing that she is up for the challenge. She is listening to her girls and breaking the cycle by getting them the necessary professional help they need. She decided to no longer run from herself, but face the demons of her past, and the oppressive present. This chapter of her healing journey was not only for her, but also for her girls.

My journey of healing met many similar stories. They made me cry, they made me question why it seemed so common. But as many stories as I was told, I could write a book just sharing others' pain. But I am more interested in the part about how to make it better. The steps people took to birth a better them.

I want to share what I continue to do to help to break the cycle in my family. In order to get to this point, I first had to live my truth, which led to many bonds of healing, and now let's review the importance of breaking these destructive cycles.

Part 3

Break the Cycle

Break it!

"Hope is being able to see that there is light despite of all of the darkness."- Desmond Tutu

When I started writing this book, I was angry at the things I learned that happened to so many people I know and love. I was angry for what happened to me. I did not realize how angry I was until I started writing. It was through the words and the emotions I was feeling as I wrote that the resentment resurfaced. But I did not like the way it felt. It took me to a place that made me question my foundation, and the people who embodied it. It is hard to heal or help others when your heart is not open. Anger is destructive to your healing process. It closes the door through which love can enter. It was through this journey of writing that the deeper understanding started. The cycle I wanted to break in the beginning of my journey was sexual abuse. But as I wrote there was so much more.

Breaking the cycle is not just about sexual abuse. It's about stopping the negative things that plagued our families for generations from continuing. Some families struggle with addiction to drugs and alcohol, physical abuse, or mental abuse. It is for us to recognize the destructive pattern and say with a conscious mind that it stops here. There is no set recipe to breaking the cycle. It's not like baking a cake. It is undertaking what you must choose to do when you are ready. You must be strategic about it and be willing to dig in, open old wounds, and feel the pain. Be prepared to pull out the skeletons from everyone's closet. There will be roadblocks and push backs. You will run into unwilling participants in the story. There will be people who are afraid of their truth and will not be happy that you are disrupting their facades. This is where the real work comes in, because some of the secret holders are long gone. Secrets have been buried, so how do you bring out the truth from generations of secrets. Somebody always knows the answers to your questions. Are you brave enough to ask? History repeats itself and ignorance can cause us to repeat the part of our past that we wish never existed. Don't be afraid to ask the hard questions and face the demons of your past.

Interview with my Abuser

The first time I spoke with him, I had a fervent desire for him to hear what I had to say. I was going to take back my control. He was going to know that what he did to me and others was damaging. And I handled that task like a boss. I stood in his face in that Jamaican hospital ward and I spoke. But as time went on and I grew, I needed not only for him to hear me, I wanted to hear what he had to say. The journey of writing this book had changed my approach. I started reaching out to everyone I knew that could connect us because in my mind I knew that he would have something profound to share. I knew that he would be able to help me with this generational puzzle. I needed that closure.

So, the day that the call came I was exhilarated! *Yes,* I thought, *now I get my chance*. As I started speaking with this sixty-year-old man to try to understand his perversion and pedophilia ways from his younger days, I realized that I was speaking to an unintelligent being. He barely understood the questions I was asking. There was no way he would have been able to put the pieces together for me like I thought. My build-up led to a disappointment. However, it was one that left me with peace. I no longer wondered what he had to say, because he truly had nothing of substance to add to my healing.

Throughout the entire conversation he thought he was speaking to another cousin, and when he spoke of me, he called me by my mother's name. I couldn't help but smile, because one of my relatives told me earlier in the week that he "was not in the right head space." This became evident during our conversation, which began with him telling me that he had just came out of the hospital where he was being treated for his diabetes. He sounded like a wounded animal as he spoke. Then I told him I had a few questions for him about why he chose the path of a pedophile. He just kept saying that was something he left behind in his younger days. When I asked him why he did it, he could not answer. I went as far as asking him if he was ever sexually abused to which he responded, "Nothing like that." So, I pressed the issue of *why?* What made you do those things? Where you born that way? He proceeded to say, "Mankind is very wicked," and he referenced one of our relatives and stated that he physically abused him, and was very "wicked", but no reference of sexual abuse. My theory was that he was either abused himself or witnessed some level of sexual abuse for him to become that person. He did mention that he saw some things and repeated how "wicked" mankind was.

Why did I think I was going to get a positive finale from the person who caused the damage? The curtain call from that screen was far from grand. It was then I realized that my closure, my healing, my end scene was dictated by me. I encourage you to not wait for anyone to close the scenes of your life. The power is all yours. You might just be waiting in vain. Or maybe you are like I was, waiting to have an unintelligible conversation with someone who didn't even realize with which one of his survivors he was speaking.

Recognize the Signs

Abusers do not come with a warning label that identifies them. You must recognize the signs and clues they give you that scream "I cannot be trusted." This is not easy, and you must trust yourself and believe your instincts and your children. When I was growing up a relative who turned out to be a victim and an abuser exhibited classic signs.

I know now what they meant. As I spoke with one of my dear cousins who experienced physical abuse at his hands, we speculated about the reasons behind his behaviors and actions.

One day while she was taking a shower, she accidentally knocked a bar of soap out the window and it fell on his newly finished woodwork. He got enraged and started yelling and cursing at a then fifteen-year-old young girl. He then shoved his way into the bathroom to continue to argue and yell at a then naked young girl. In defense she yelled at him asking if he was coming in the bathroom to "rape" her. His rage turned into violence and he attacked the naked child leaving bruises and marks on her body. This incident not only left physical marks on her body, but it bruised her soul for a lifetime. When the arresting officer came, it was his brother who saved him from jail that dark day.

Thirty years later when my dear cousin shared this story the hurt and pain was as fresh as the day it happened to her. Yet together we were able to analyze it and realize that the word "rape" triggered the violence. Maybe he thought she knew and his attack on her was to shut her up. We must not be silenced. We must share our pain so that we can save a life.

This relative was always angry, he yelled and beat on the children in his path. He abused animals just for being in his way. He bullied his victims into being afraid to speak up. I remember one of his victims being a depressed child that the other children made fun of because they did not understand his plight, and because he hid his tragic story. He hid under the beds, and in cages with our animals throughout the day. It was a strange behavior and none of the adults had the insight to recognize that it was a cry for help. I remembered when I first learned Blake's tragic story, I got angry and woke up in tears because I imagined the fear, hurt, and violation of my dear cousin.

Sexual abuse does not just affect the abused. It affects everyone around them. When one of our relatives found out what happened to Blake, he cried for days. He expressed remorse and guilt and stated that he had "failed us". He wished he knew and could have changed the hands of time. His tears sounded like mourning for a person he thought he knew, and helplessness for not being able to save a child's life from being tainted.

The most interesting thing about this story, was that after the story broke out, everyone had something that they knew that was never spoken about. Some people said they heard stories about Blake's abuser being abused by the neighbor. Others talked about his Boys Scout leader being a predator and leading some of the boys to his house often, while others talked about his incest behavior with some female relatives. All these actions where signs of something gone wrong, yet no one spoke up. I know this story is deeper than the surface stories we were told. I know that the generations of sexual deviance are embedded in the walls of the house, and the soil of the land that we grew up on. There are many more stories to tell and sometimes I see them in my dreams.

I understand why a person in so much pain and turmoil would meet such a tragic end. It is not only the potential victims we want to protect. We must help those who have been victimized to heal and work on not becoming an abuser. This is huge part of breaking the cycle of sexual abuse. God did not create abusers, they were made from hurt, pain and a sense of self hate. When you can identify your abuser as a prior victim, you have come a long way on your healing journey. When I think of my abusers, I also think of the victims they were. I imagine how different the story would be if they were surrounded with love and taught how to love themselves despite of the traumatic situations they were exposed to.

It's Your Choice

The way you choose to work on breaking the cycle will be completely up to you. This is a personal mission, and no one recipe will work for everyone. Remember as I stated before you are making life changing decisions that will not only affect you, but your children, and your grandchildren. It is your family's legacy that you are creating. When you work on breaking the cycle you are demolishing a destructive family curse and creating a constructive family legacy. It will not be easy, but it must be done with deliberate actions, a conscious mind, and an open heart.

My work started long before I knew what I was really doing. I was in my mid-twenties when all that I had suppressed started coming back to me. The tears would come but I would be uncertain as to why. The healing process was triggered by a lost love. I had fallen in love with a boy in college that was unavailable both because he apparently had a girlfriend who I knew nothing about, and because he was also lost, and uncertain. When the reality slapped me in the face, the search for self-love got started.

I wondered why I was hurting so deeply for someone who I knew was being deceptive. The love that I had longed for was not coming from the people I had surrounded myself with. I was seeking external love because I had not yet learned how to love myself. I did not know that I didn't love myself because I had no idea how that was supposed to look. No one taught me how to love myself. I was deep in guilt and shame, those negative emotions that can create havoc in our lives. All I knew was what I felt at that moment, and none of what I felt acknowledged my past that had abandonment, sexual abuse, mommy issues and daddy issues neatly tucked away as if they were not part of my story.

I was beautifully broken! I was well put together, with hair always well done, clothes neatly tucked, and shoes that carried the latest brand name. I smiled through it as if it never happened. But looking back, my choices in men and how I let them treat me told the true tale. It was as if I allowed myself to be violated again, but this time with consent. It was a breach of my body and my soul, as I often cried without understanding the depth of the tears. I was beautiful, but I was in pain! I was beautiful, but I had a longing. I was beautiful, but I was broken.

There is always a turning point in our lives, and mine happened when my college love looked me in the face and denied me. I had been pushed to the side by my mother and father and was left to figure it out. It was so damn difficult to navigate, even when I made it look easy. And here I was again being denied and pushed to the side. It was then that I knew I had work to do. I might have been beautiful, but my insecurities must have been so obvious that these men thought it was justified to reject me.

It was through these devastating moments that I started working on myself, yet even then I did not have full awareness as to what I was truly working to fix. I made many more relationship mistakes before I started using the power of discernment. As I read many books, I sought peace by enjoying being still and alone. It started to become clearer that it was my choice to either live with the baggage of shame and guilt or work to find the truest form of love--self-love. Broken people get to put the pieces back together exactly how they desire it to be. We become the master of our destiny, no one else, just us this time. We get a do over. What will it look like? How will you make it count?

Invest in Yourself

It was during my journey in self-discovery that I found Iyanla Vanzant's work. Her books spoke to me as if they were written just for me. I became hooked on her work and bought all the books that she wrote in the late nineties. *One Day my Soul Just Opened Up* served as a daily dose of strength, love, and devotion. The workbook within the pages allowed me to write down my feelings in accordance with her guidance, and I wrote what I feared, what I realized, and what I accepted. It was this book that first taught me about reason, season, and lifetime relationships.

It was then that I started being able to let go of unproductive relationships with barely a thought. It was through this process I realized the importance of keeping people around me who supported my vision. I started easily removing myself from people who, as I would say, threw me "off balance." These people included friends and family members. It really didn't matter who you were, because my journey was more important.

Iyanla's work didn't stop with that book--there was, *Yesterday, I Cried* and *In the Meantime*. As I read her story of being a teenage mother, and of her struggles, she gave me hope that one day I would feel whole. I knew I would be able to share my story and live my calling of helping others. I remember signing up for a retreat and driving to Upstate New York from Maryland in hopes of seeing Iyanla Vanzant speak. This did not work out, but my disappointment did not stop me. I continued to embrace her work and stayed on my path.

My journey started with Iyanla Vanzant, but continued with Louise L. Hay who, through her words on the pages of her book *You Can Heal Your Life,* reminded me that I was completely responsible for me. She taught me that the only way to change my life and become fulfilled would be to change my thoughts. I learned to think what I want to be and practice the actions that I want to see. She focused on forgiveness of self and others. Her encouragement of forgiveness resonated with me because I had so many to forgive. My Mother, father, abusers, and later in life the very people who I thought were taking great care of me. Louise L. Hay wrote about making sure we release our negative emotions so that we prevent them from building up and cause our bodies illness. It was many years later that those words were validated during a message from heaven.

Then there was Deepak Chopra's *The Seven Spiritual Laws of Success* where I learned to become more in tuned with the universe and listened more intently to my inner voice. Through Chopra's book I understood more about what I was attracting in my life by way of my thinking, and my doing. I became an avid reader, and I knew that through the knowledge from these books, coupled with therapy, I would be able to make it through this journey. The journey I was on back then was self-serving. It was about me, understanding me. I know now that it was a necessary part of my healing, and it was a step closer to breaking the cycle.

Use your Gift

When I was ten years old, my grandmother took me to orientation at the new school that I would start in the fall. I believe it was a hot August day in Jamaica. As we stepped off the bus and crossed Constant Spring Road to the gates of Immaculate Conception High School, it occurred to me that I had seen this place many times in my dreams. As I shared with my grandmother the awe of this place that I had never been but knew so well, she said "you have the gift, baby." As a ten-year-old girl I had no clue what my grandmother was talking about. The "gift" she explained, was the gift of dreams, the gift of knowing.

My intuitive spirit served me well throughout my years, but only when I paid attention and listened. I knew that it was truly a gift when I was able to clearly see the things, and people, that would cross my path in my dreams. They were less about symbolism, and more about preparing me for what's to come. Now as an adult, I am grateful for such a gift because it has guided me throughout adulthood and has led me to my wonderful husband, and an enriched life purpose.

During my turbulent times of seeking love from all the wrong people, I always knew when they were wrong for me. I would get messages through dreams, and sometimes just a strong sense of knowing, yet I would carry on. This stubbornness led to many mishaps that didn't stop in my college years, it lasted for a full decade after. It was as if I did not trust myself and what I knew. I ignored my spiritual guidance that came from within, and I paid dearly. It was a long road to the point when I acknowledged that I was being guided all this time and I was not receptive. When I started listening and paying attention, the love of my life was sent to me. I had ignored that message the first time, and two years later it was so clear there was no denying it.

We met two years prior to the day I had a divine realization that he was the man I would spend the rest of my life with. Back then my friends saw the connection, and I told them they were crazy. But there was no denying it the second time around.

I had many spiritual validations that led me to my husband. One day as I was having a conversation with him, I asked him to help me pick a three-digit pin number for a password I needed when calling him. When he casually gave me the same three-digit number I had been seeing for many years before that day, I was persuaded. However, it was the dream of my grandmother placing her hand on his head and telling me "take care of him" that sealed the deal. I knew then that they were heavenly signs. I knew then that I had enough and was not willing to continue down the same path, and so I prayed. But this time my prayer was specific. When you allow yourself to be vulnerable in the eyes of God, the clarity is unreal.

Recognizing My Beauty

A therapist once told me that the situation I was in at the time was like "giving a pearl to a pig." This was a statement that stayed with me for a long time, since it happened twenty-six years ago. But what made the comment so special, was that she referred to me as a pearl. The dictionary defines a pearl as "a hard, lustrous spherical mass, typically white or bluish-gray, formed within the shell of a pearl oyster or other bivalve mollusk and highly prized as a gem."

Oh my, I was a "highly prized gem." No one had ever described me that way, nor did I see myself in that manner.

However, as I continued my journey, I measured myself against that "prized gem." I used it as my benchmark, and every time I would feel hurt, I would say "what a pig!"

Recognizing what you are worth and using it as a standard is a valuable tool to anyone on a journey to self-love. This realization never left me, and I continued to feel like a prize. I added other precious pretty things to my portfolio--a rose, royalty, rainbows, and other things that shine bright. What will be your benchmark of beauty and wholeness? What will be that thing that makes you want to put in the work and be well?

Replace the Doors

Before my journey of healing started, my dreams about closing the doors to the house I spent my formative years in came often. The evidence that I was well on my way to healing came when that recurring dream ended. The dream I had that put a stake in the healing process was clear. In my dreams I was an adult and I returned to the house and I was having a profound discussion with my grandmother and her sister. I had replaced all the doors with new doors that could lock. I told them that I spared no expense and bought them the best doors. However, there was a problem with replacing the front door.

I could not find a door to fit the front of the house and I was unable to change that door. I argued with the matriarchs about the situation. Why couldn't I replace the front door? When I woke up that profound dream made sense of the nonsensical childhood. The predators were welcomed. They lived in the house and walked through the front door. There was no way I could replace that door. Not even in my dreams.

The house I had jurisdiction to protect was the house that my family and I live in. This was my sanctuary, my safe zone, my Zen place. Those of you who are invited are vetted. But sometimes the wolf is in sheep's clothing. The day I had a sweet young girl express that someone I trusted and loved had disrespected my home by violating her within the walls I considered a "safe zone," it took me back many years for many days.

A person I trusted and knew for a very long time and was always invited to my home, made advances to my niece in my home while she was in my care. It was significant for me since I prayed about keeping my doors closed to these types of situations. I thought I could trust him, and deep down never imagined I would have dealt with such an ordeal. But even the most aware person still must be careful. On that day I had to tell someone I love and trusted that they were no longer welcomed through my doors. I verbally fought for her and made sure she understood the importance of speaking up. On that day she learned many lessons, but the most important one was that when she spoke her truth, someone was there to support and protect her. Your beauty does not give anyone the right to violate you. On that day through my anger and disappointment I showed my children the importance of protecting each other, and never allowing a wolf to open the closed front door of our home.

None of us are immune from these types of situations even when we think we are staying aware. The truth is even with the love I had for this young man I would not have left him alone with my niece because I had learned the hard way about trust. But on this day, I was not given the choice. He went to house without my knowledge and she was there alone.

One of the toughest things I had to do was share with a mom that her child experienced unwanted advances and perversion while she was under my care. I cried through the entire conversation and had a feeling of failure. "Not in my house," I cried. I could not breathe--I felt like my entire world was upside down. I remember the kindness and love that came from the other side of the phone, "I am so sorry that happened, I can just imagine the memories and feelings it brought back."

When you surround yourself with an awesome support system, you can walk through any storm.

Your Sister's Keeper

While in college, as I longed for normality and a sense of family, I attempted to pledge a sorority. Because of internal turmoil the sorority was going through, me and my line sisters ended up being left in the cold without the Greek letters we worked for. But I should have known because even at that young age, the pledging process went against everything I believed in. I wanted the sisterhood but looking back I think the process was counterproductive. But what God had in store for me was already present in my life, that bond of sisters who took the journey with me then kept going with me through many phases of my life. The ups and downs, the joys the pain. I don't think anyone knows me better than these beautiful ladies I have grown to call sisters. I recreated my family with this group of women who became my lifetime sisters. No, this was not done by way of a sorority--it was by plain divine, pure love that we were brought together. Like any family we had our ups and downs, but we always came back together. This thirty-year friendship and sisterhood have seen us through some of the most challenging times in our lives. We all needed each other at some point. If I had an important engagement like my birthday (smile), my sisters were there to help me celebrate. Everything was good in the world. They became the functional family I never had. We spoke openly, we loved unconditionally, and we supported each other without reservations.

When I was in therapy, I spoke of my circle of sisters often, and my therapist said to me "do you realize what you did?" She said, "You created a new family." And she was right; these women have a special space in my heart, and although life has us spread around the country, we find ways to celebrate each other and the sisterhood we formed thirty years ago. Time and distance separated us but love always brings us back together.

Your journey of healing cannot be done alone. You must be surrounded with love and support. You will need a shoulder to cry on, an outlet for laughter, and just that person that you know you can depend on.

I found myself practicing "my sister's keeper" throughout my life. I remember when one of my biological sisters visited with me when she was 13 years old, and I was in my late twenties. All I wanted to do was make sure she was whole. I wanted to make sure she practiced self-love. I went out and I bought her a book for teenagers by Iyanla Vanzant, *Don't Give It Away*. It was personal because she was my sister, and we shared the same father. My sister and I relived that visit recently, and it was awesome to hear her say she remembered it all. She remembered that book and said it was exactly what she needed at that time.

I had a couple of cousins that I spoiled. They would come around and we would have fun times such as shopping sprees and many other awesome experiences. I always wanted to have the younger girls around. A part of me just wanted to protect them and make sure they knew what they were worth. They knew they could come around me to escape whatever they were going through. I was their support. Around me they had a voice.

Messages from Heaven

One of the most enlightening day I had in my life was the day I laid next to my grandfather and comforted him while he transitioned from this earth. That day intensified my spiritual belief system and changed my thinking about death. I have always known that my loved ones who left earth moved on to a place of peace. But somehow, I knew they were close. Sometimes I could feel their presence as if they never left, and often I received messages through my dreams. Before my grandfather left this earth, there was my grandmother, and then her sister who transitioned before him.

This event was a two-week ordeal. My family planned to spend Christmas with my mother and my grandfather, but while we were on our way, I received a phone call.

My mother was frantically trying to explain to me that grandfather was in the emergency room. Here explanation was filled with tears and I started to panic. I started thinking my grandfather was going to die before I got to spend Christmas with him. It was just three months prior I had to break the news about his brother's tragic death, and I promised him that I would be there for him. I promised that I would be by his side and he would be surrounded with love. *But I wouldn't get to fulfill my promise if I was still on the road driving to him.* My thoughts were running wild.

Since it wasn't his time to leave this earth, I did get to see my grandfather. It wasn't the ideal Christmas since I spend that night in the hospital with my grandfather, holding his hand and talking about whatever he wanted to talk about. I felt sad and joy mixed. I was sad he was not well and based on the diagnosis he wasn't going to be well again. Yet I felt joy that I was there by his side just like I promised.

The day after Christmas my grandfather was sent home under hospice care, and I was there until a week later. Throughout that week my he delivered many messages and spoke of things that was out of this world. He spoke of things that didn't connect until almost a year later. That Sunday morning when God decided it was time to take him back is etched in my memory because it was profound. I laid in the bed with my grandfather and I sang his favorite song, *I surrender all*. He took his last breath after I told him I loved him, and it would be alright to go. I remember the peaceful last breath. It was surreal! Although his transition was calm, my reaction to him no longer breathing was disconcerted. I soon found the peace I needed to handle the loss I felt.

It was a few weeks after my grandfather passed away that I started getting a fervid need to see a medium. I started getting a strong sense that he had something to share with me. Although I researched mediums within that year, it would take me six years before I spoke with one. One day I was led to speak to a spiritual adviser/medium. She was not the Hollywood medium, but she sure did bring me messages from heaven.

After I heard the heart-breaking news about Blake's abuse, I needed to speak with his abuser who had passed away. I reached out to a spiritual adviser who used her gift and connected me to my loved ones including this man. I learned a lot that day. Some things I already knew, and some had me in awe. Sometimes we have abusers who have passed, and we never got a chance to confront them. But it's never too late to get the closure you deserve.

During this session I talked with my loved ones. I needed answers and they were able to give them to me. They expressed great remorse and regret for their actions. One simply said that "hurt people, hurt people." My relative had experienced his own issues with abuse growing up. It seemed that this traumatic pattern that carried on to the next generation of boys in my grandparent's household was because of an unbroken cycle of abuse. I also needed to know from my grandmother why she did nothing about the web of sexual abuse that filled every corner of her house.

Her answer was that she kept the secrets to avoid bringing shame to the family. She said that the culture would not have been accepting. However, she did state that because she kept so many secrets it made her sick and caused her to die at an early age. Don't get me wrong I loved my grandmother then and cherishes her memory now. She was old school and ignorant to how she should have handled the many things that she kept secret. She protected people in the moment without understanding the long-term effects and consequences. She resolved situations the way her parents resolved them. It was learned behavior and a cultural mishap. Her encouraging words to me through this medium gave me strength. Although this matriarch was no longer living, I felt the need to explain and gain permission for speaking my truth.

But it was when my grandfather came through and shared that on the day of his passing, he knew I was there. He wanted to thank me for being there. He said he placed his hand on my shoulder to comfort me when I became saddened. I always wondered if my grandfather knew I was there like I promised, and I got my answer.

On this day I learned that I must continue my path and speak out so that I can save as many lives as possible. Silence and secrets will not break a generation of abuse. We must go against the naysayers and remove the destructive legacy. We must free our minds and let set your soul free. We must listen to our children. We must encourage them to speak out.

Step Out of Yourself

Another important factor in breaking the cycle is the practice of selflessness. Share your story with those around you, especially your children. It is important to give them the raw truth about life and how to combat it. This is not to taint their young minds, but to equip them with nuggets that will one day save their lives. Selflessness is also about the time you spend with your children. Let them know you love them no matter what. Children must be heard. They have a lot to say. The moment they feel like they don't have a voice, and you are not listening, you have created a way for those monsters to climb out of the closets.

The fallout might be that they will not speak again until the damage is already done, and sometimes they never speak. If you invest in your children the way you would a stock, constantly monitoring their progress, making course corrections when necessary, you will later be able to celebrate the return on investment.

My parenting was severely influenced by my years growing up. I was left to navigate some interesting situations, and in hindsight it was like being dropped at sea without a life vest. Once I made the decision to have a family, I vowed to be a different type of parent. I wanted to give my children what they needed to make it through their growing years. A lot of which was self-taught and based on instincts since I never directly experienced it. They need someone to understand their fears and tell them it's going to be alright, someone to provide them with tools to overcome the moments of defeat. They want to be celebrated for their moments of triumph and encouraged to keep it going. I have been known to go a bit overboard, but that was just me trying to get it right.

As a young child I had a fear of lizards. I am not sure what started this dread for these little creatures, but I would jump out of my shoes when I met them. I remember there was one that lived behind the tank in the bathroom which caused me to panic every time I needed to have a personal moment. It was moments like those were I needed the support and nurturing of a parent. Instead I got a teasing and reaction that my deepest fear was trivial. No one took the time to understand why I was afraid. In contrast, my young daughter loves these little creepy crawlers and even wants to help me get over my fear. Looking back, some of my fears did have some humor in them, but I had no one to help me laugh. Like the time I climbed the Ackee tree and jumped down and stepped on one of mother hen's chick and it died. That gave me nightmares of the hen chasing me for a very long time.

There are times when we all wonder why we are struggling with certain fears, and it's no wonder we sometimes leave goodness on the table. We sometimes can't see through the fog of our fears that were developed during childhood. It is a sad contribution to the broken cycle when a child does not have the nurturing of parents that comforts their fears. It leads us to where we are today.

I have a need to always know where my children are, and who they are with. This is a critical point of my parenting. Growing up there were many times only I knew my location. Some of these situations could have caused me terrible harm. To say I had an angel is an understatement. It is my belief that I had an army of angels. I have vivid memories of me as a child hiding behind the door of my grandmother's bedrooms. I don't remember what I was hiding from, but I distinctly remember that within that moment I wished I had my mother. That memory has stayed with me for my lifetime. Having the presence of my mother was a deep need for me as a child. I can only imagine that it is a deep longing for other children to have their parents.

When I was in college my best friend and I made some profound statements about what our lives would be like when we were older. We vowed that we would not have children out of wedlock. We wanted the picket fence and the husband. We talked about breaking the single mother, absenteeism father cycle we had seen in our families. Looking back at those talks I realize that we were aware then that our lives had a void. I am not saying that children cannot be great with just one parent. I am talking about breaking that cycle that was present in our families.

I am unapologetic about the way I

parent because I give to my children what I truly needed in my life at their age. These are some of the things that I hope will aid in breaking destructive cycles. I use the word hope because we can work as hard as possible and put in all the parenting hours, but our children are not always with us and those gaps can create unknown issues. Even knowing that, parents must work effortlessly to fill the time with their children with love, lessons learned, laughter, and dance. Create the memories that give them something to come back to, a place they can truly call home, where memories bring a smile to their faces and not tears.

The Journey

During my journey I met many women and men who shared their stories, simply because I was able to share mine. *Daring Greatly,* Brene Brown's book stated, "We cannot experience empathy if we are not connecting." It was through the pages of *Daring Greatly* that I understood the true meaning, and importance, of vulnerability. I had also shared my story with close friends, and relatives, but understanding that through connection comes healing, I started using social media to talk to a broader audience. These were people I worked with, and who had only seen the well put together me. But I knew I served a bigger purpose, and I needed to share my story with others.

Brene Brown, defined vulnerability as "uncertainty, risk, and emotional exposure." As she listed the way other people saw vulnerability, she broke it down to it being more like "truth" and "courage." Here I was again at a different place in my journey where another fabulous author's work made a great impact. Now my journey was no longer self-serving. It was no longer just about breaking the cycle for my children and my grandchildren. It was time to serve a bigger population. Tell my truth, then I would be able to live my truth, and through this I will help others to break their silence and break the cycle.

I have learned many lessons during my journey of healing, and even more during this process of writing. The biggest one was that it had to start with myself. It started with me wanting to be a happier person. Then I wanted to feel whole and forgive others. Then I wanted to break the cycle for the family that I wanted but felt crippled to start. Then I wanted to be the best mom, and wife. And now, I want to make the biggest impact, which is be at service for those who need me. I intend to save a life one person at a time.

I leave you with a charge that will be one of the boldest steps you might make in your life. Change your family's legacy by doing the following:

- ☐ Be willing to do the work
- ☐ Recognize the signs
- ☐ Give your children a voice
- ☐ Choose to change the story
- ☐ Listen to your inner voice
- ☐ Create a supportive community
- ☐ Use your pain to help others
- ☐ Seek professional help
- ☐ Be BOLD! Be FEARLESS! Be WHOLE!
- ☐ Start LIVING!

Letter to my Abusers

Dear Pathetic You,

At one point I thought you won. I was sure that I was broken and could not be put back together. I even pretended that what you did to me did not really happen. But my dreams kept reminding me that you were there. I kept growing physically, mentally, and spiritually despite your violations. I wondered if one day I would be able to have a healthy sexual relationship without you being a third wheel. I wondered if the guilt and shame you caused would ever go away. You made it very difficult for me to build self-worth and self-esteem for a very long time. I just couldn't imagine life without you. I was carrying you around like a bad habit that I could not kick. But one day I took a chance and I spoke about your disgusting ways and it felt good. So, I decided to try again, and again. Each time I spoke of you I felt something being returned to me. My love for self, my desire to help others to never have to stay silent. My desire is to save another child from dealing with you.

I don't know if anyone ever told you how disgusting you are. But I want to share something else with you that I don't believe you have been told before. What happened to you was not your fault. When you were victimized you had no support. You had no one to listen to you, no one to love you and tell you that you were not broken. So, you kept the secret until it decayed in your soul and created your predatory ways. You have hurt so many that you don't even remember who they are. But they sure remember you. You creep into every aspect of their lives. You are the recurring nightmare. You have been trying to mask your hurt and your pain for so long. Why couldn't you have used a more productive outlet? I don't blame you for what happened to you, but I damn sure blame you for what happened to me. You could have done better.

I want to share with you that you have been exposed. The world knows who you are. The world knows what you did. It is no longer in the dark because I have shared it with many. You no longer have power over me. I took it back and shared it with some others like me. Together we are going to make sure the light stays on. My children know about you and what you did. Yes, I shared it! I wanted them to know who you are so that they can turn on the spotlight when you come around. Did you think I was going to allow this behavior to continue in my family? You hope I did. Don't be surprised, somebody had to break the cycle. I smile a lot now, my anger has been redirected, my guilt and shame turned to love. I know exactly who I am. I have never been surer. I am not afraid of the dark, but I prefer to walk in my truth.

Sincerely, Survivor

Epilogue

When you regained your power from any type of abuse and realize you have been wronged, you must try hard to prevent it from happening again. This is when my heightened sense of protect yourself and others went into overdrive. This is when I learned to listen to my inner voice. This is when I recognized "a sheep in wolves clothing." I once had a boyfriend that long after we dated told me that he admired me because he was not able to pull the wool over my eyes. Most importantly I took this heightened sense of knowing to my workplace. This was where many lessons were learned, friendships grew, bosses came, and bosses left. But the most important part of knowing was when I drummed up the courage to walk away. I walked away because the environment became another form of abuse and I was adamant that I was not going to take shit from anyone ever again. That included people who signed off on thousands of dollars. I was not going to allow myself to be diminished, demeaned, used, lied on, lied about for money. Especially by so-called leaders with shallow souls and short visions. It was during this time that the idea of "Authentic Leadership" came to mind. The idea of a book was born because I saw the need for leaders to view their employees as humans with challenges that surpassed performance indicators and revenue. When you regain that power, you must take it through the different facets of your life. Don't back down! Recognize when it is good and celebrate! And dump it when it is bad. Work feverishly to prevent yourself from becoming a victim again.

Giving Thanks

First, I want to thank my friend Deshaune Wiley for giving me the courage and motivating me to write this book. The day you gave me that journal started a different level of my healing process. For that I must say thank you. There were so many people involved in making this a reality. I wrote the book, but not without the stories from other brave survivors. There were those who had no idea that they were encouraging me to make one of the bravest moves of my life when they shared the most intimate part of themselves with me. Their willingness to be vulnerable touched me deeply and inadvertently aided in my healing. For this I am sincerely grateful.

I want to thank my friend Magan Thomas for editing my manuscript and giving me the most encouraging and honest feedback. Magan thank you for taking the time even during a difficult period for your family. Thank you to Nathan Dodds for putting my vision into art and making my book cover exactly what I desired. He did this while juggling a newborn. Thanks to Coach Stacey Croston, and Kiana Kee for being my test readers. You ladies are fantastic for always believing in me. I must thank my Aunt Jen, Aunt Leslene, and cousin Tally for moral support and understanding. Allowing me to talk, cry and laugh through the pain made a huge difference.

The cousins in my life, I love you all for being strong enough to survive a disturbing childhood. I wrote this book for all of us. You have a voice and silence is not acceptable. I encourage you to put a stake in the ground for your children and your grandchildren. Change the legacy! Create one that will make you proud.

I am indebted to the Carr household for allowing me to make drastic changes and share my life with hopes of helping as many people as I can. To my most patient, calm, and loving husband, I love you for supporting my dreams no matter what they are. For loving me with all my flaws. For being a life partner that can bring calm to any storm. I love you.

I want to thank my readers for choosing my book. I am proud of you for tackling this subject and I encourage you to pass it on and save a life.

I thank God for giving me the divine messages that led me to have break throughs both for myself and others. God spoke and I listened!

www.ingramcontent.com/pod-product-compliance
Lightning Source LLC
Chambersburg PA
CBHW021937290426
44108CB00012B/870